Essential
Ayurveda

Presented by:

SREE SANKARA COMMUNITY FOR
AYURVEDA CONSCIOUSNESS LTD

Kerala - India
www.sreesankara.com

Salim Pushpanath

Dr. Vijayachandradas

Jacob Philip

Essential Ayurveda

Photography & Concept: Salim Pushpanath

Consultant Physician: Dr.Vijayachandradas,
Sree Sankara Ayurveda Hospital, Changanacherry, Kerala, India

Text: Jacob Philip

Pre-press & Color Management: Brijilal

Production Co-ordinator: Thomas Kurian

Design: Dinkar & Deepak Devaraj

Pre-press: www.colortone.co.in

For overseas rights and sales, please contact the publisher.

Printed and bound by Times Offset (M) Sdn Bhd, Malaysia

Location courtsy:
    Ayurveda centre   - Aquaserene Backwater Resort, Kollam, Kerala
    Herbal garden   - Sree Sankara Gardens, Anakkara, Kumily

Published by Salim Pushpanath
DEE BEE INFO PUBLICATIONS
"Pushpanath" Malloossery, Kottayam - 686 041. Kerala, India.
Tel: 00 481 2391429, 2302799.
Email:salimpushpanath@gmail.com
www.salimpushpanath.com
www.dbventure.com

Printed in Malyasia

www.dbventure.com
ISBN 81-88000-13-2

9 788188 000135
Essential Ayurveda
Rs.395/-

Lord Dhanwantari
(God of Ayurveda)

Ayurveda – a gift to mankind

Ayurveda is a holistic health science that evolved down the ages in ancient India some 5000 years ago advocating a way of life in combination with diagnosing and curing ailments in perfect harmony with Mother Nature. Derived from Sanskrit Ayurveda is a compound word that implies two connected ideas – *"the science of life,"* and *"the art of living. "*

The mythical origin of Ayurveda is a fascinating story in itself. According to ancient Hindu mythology the gods invoked Dhanwantari the Lord of Ayurveda from the oceans for the elixir of life by churning it with a mountain for a rod and Vasuki the giant serpent for a rope. However just as Dhanwantari emerged from the waters the demons snatched the elixir of life from him and it was only after a wily battle of wits with the demons that the gods were able to retrieve the nectar of life!

Ayurveda was originally a Hindu medical system and textbooks refer to Maharishi Bharadwaj as being instrumental in compiling this fascinating health science and showcasing it as an independent branch of medicine. Ayurveda was however quickly adopted by almost all existing religious groups and began spreading to far away places such as China, Afghanistan and Persia. Ayurveda developed at about the same time as Buddhism and Hinduism and replaced earlier ideas on disease and healing that were written down in religious texts such as the Atharva-Veda. It is the earliest and most comprehensive system of healthcare known to mankind and has managed to not only survive till date but is even challenging modern medicine in many ways and attracting ardent followers to this commonsensical way of life from around the world. Ayurveda is indeed a gift from the gods to mankind.

Based on the primordial Indian philosophy of *"Live and Let Live,"* there are several aspects to Ayurveda, which distinguishes it from contemporary healthcare systems. It focuses on establishing and maintaining the balance of the life's energies within us, rather than focusing on individual symptoms. It recognizes the unique constitutional differences of all individuals and recommends different regimens for different types of people. Although two people may appear to have the same outward symptoms, their energetic constitutions may be very different and therefore call for very different remedies.

The basic hypothesis of Ayurveda is that the entire cosmos or universe is part of one singular absolute. Everything that exists in the vast external universe (macrocosm) also appears in the internal cosmos of the human body (microcosm). The human body consisting of 50 million to 100 million cells when healthy, is in harmony, self-perpetuating and self-correcting just as the universe is. The ancient Ayurveda text, Charaka, says, "Man is the epitome of the universe. Within man, there is as much diversity as in the world outside. Similarly, the outside world is as diverse as human beings themselves." In other words, all human beings are a living microcosm of the universe and the universe is a living macrocosm of the human beings.

Ayurveda postulates that all intelligence and wisdom flows from one Absolute source "Paramatma." Health is a result of the manifestation of the Absolute acting through the laws of Mother Nature. It promotes harmony between man and the universe by proposing a life of balance in synchrony with the laws of Mother Nature. According to Ayurveda, there are certain fundamental energies that regulate all natural processes on both a macrocosmic and microcosmic levels. These energies that regulate the entire universe are also believed to control human physiology. Ayurveda is holistic; it views the human being as a whole and advises ways and means of living one's life rightfully attaining physical, mental and spiritual wellness optimally. It is applicable to all living things, as indicated by its name, the science of life. Vedic sciences attribute life to more things than we normally do - the things such as air, wind, fire, the earth, planets, stars, etcetera are all thought to possess conscience like living beings.

Ayurveda emphasises prevention of disease, rejuvenation of our body systems, and longevity of life. The insightful assertion and promise of Ayurveda is that through certain practices, not only can we thwart – for example, coronary disorders and make our migraines disappear but we can also better understand ourselves and the world around us, live long healthy lives in balance and harmony, achieve our fullest potential expressing our true inner-self on a daily basis.

Ayurveda provides an integrated approach to preventing and treating illness through lifestyle modification and natural therapies. It is based on the view that the diverse elements, forces, and principles that make up Mother Nature is also evident in human beings. In Ayurveda, the mind or consciousness and the body or physical mass not only complement and influence each other but also in unison constitutes a human being. The universal consciousness is a super intelligent bundle of vivacious energy that helps us perceive through our five senses the physical world.

Vidari
Lat: Ipoma nil
Malayalam: Palmuthakku
Useful part: Tuber
Main Indications:
Lactogenic, Constipation.

Ayurvedic philosophy and practices link us to every aspect of ourselves and remind us that we are in union with every facet of nature, each other, and the entire universe. There can be no mental health without physical health, and vice versa. In Ayurveda, symptoms and diseases that could be categorized as mental thoughts or feelings are just as important as symptoms and diseases of the physical body. Both are due to imbalances within a person, and restoring the natural balance mentally and physically is the right treatment. In Ayurveda your whole life and lifestyle must be in harmony before you can enjoy true health and happiness. Lifestyle alterations combined with a therapeutic approach is an atypical Ayurvedic approach to holistic wellness.

India is perhaps the only country where Ayurvedic practitioners receive state-recognized institutionalised training similar to their allopathic counterparts. Modern research has proved beyond a shadow of doubt the therapeutic effects of Ayurveda and innumerable published studies have documented reductions in cardiovascular disease risk factors, including blood pressure, cholesterol and reaction to stress - to name a few of the more common ailments - amongst individuals who underwent Ayurvedic treatment plans.

Laboratory and clinical studies on Ayurvedic herbal preparations and other therapies have shown them to have a range of potentially beneficial effects for preventing and treating certain cancers, infectious disease, chronic disorders such as diabetes, arthritis

and controlling the aging process. Mechanisms underlying these effects may include free-radical scavenging effects, immune system modulation, brain neurotransmitter modulation, and hormonal effects.

The uniqueness of every human being

Ayurveda views each and every person as unique, with a unique mind-body constitution and a unique set of life circumstances, all of which must be considered in determining the healing approaches and recommendations for everyday life. This is similar to the view of modern science where the structure of the DNA makes every human being unique and an entity unto him or herself.

According to Ayurveda as the physical and metaphysical constitutions differ from person to person the approach to viewing an individual's ailment and treating it varies according to the constitution of the individual. This means that in order to be healthy, you need to eat certain foods that are beneficial for your body type and stay away from others. Your exercise program must be personally suitable as well. Your constitution determines very much about you - your body, your personality, even your interpersonal relations with fellow human beings in society.

Agnimantha
Lat: Premna serratifolia
Malayalam: Munja
Useful part: Root bark, Leaves
Main Indications:Obesity,
Inflemmation, Toxins.

The theoretical side of Ayurveda provides insights into how to live one's life in harmony with nature and natural laws and rhythms. Its practical side - specifically its guidelines for an intelligently regulated diet and daily routine, its techniques for stress management, and its exercises for increased fitness and alertness-help us take control of our lives and develop radiant health.

The central goal of Ayurveda is nothing less than a state of perfect health, for the individual and for society and the environment as well, in which every man and woman is inwardly in balance and outwardly in harmony with the environment and the laws of nature.

According to Ayurveda, nature is permeated by intelligence. Intelligent laws govern the growth of all living things; puppies grow into dogs and acorns into oak trees. Indeed, laws of nature regulate everything, from the miniscule world of whirling atoms to the colossal world of galaxies.

The human body is part of nature, as we discussed before as a microcosm of the universe, and when it runs perfectly, as it was designed to run, it can be perfectly healthy. It is trying to be perfectly healthy all the time, using its innate self-healing, self-regulating ability as it strives for a perfect homeostatic balance. But we repeatedly interfere.

Nature has set us up with all the equipment we need to be perfectly healthy. Health is our natural state, and ill health is unnatural. Every day we are exposed to literally millions of bacteria, viruses, allergens, even carcinogens, and yet our immune system has the intelligence and skill to deal with all those invaders and keep us healthy. However, when stress, inadequate nutrition, or just fatigue weakens the immune system, those same invaders may produce disease.

Each second our bodies are adjusting to countless thousands of changing parameters in its effort to maintain the homeostatic balance. No matter what comes along to upset the balance, the body knows its own nature, knows what ideal temperature it should be and the correct chemistry that's needed to maintain, and keeps referring back to that blueprint to maintain proper balance.

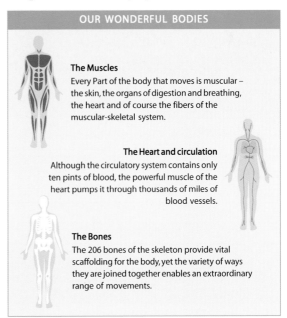

OUR WONDERFUL BODIES

The Muscles
Every Part of the body that moves is muscular – the skin, the organs of digestion and breathing, the heart and of course the fibers of the muscular-skeletal system.

The Heart and circulation
Although the circulatory system contains only ten pints of blood, the powerful muscle of the heart pumps it through thousands of miles of blood vessels.

The Bones
The 206 bones of the skeleton provide vital scaffolding for the body, yet the variety of ways they are joined together enables an extraordinary range of movements.

The Concept of Self

The **Self**, as this inner dimension of our nature is called in Ayurveda, is the central point of our being, the hub of the wheel. It is the true inner centre of our diversified lives. Thought, feelings, speech, action, and relationships all originate here, deep within the personality. The process of self-referral, or looking within to experience the Self can spontaneously enhance the whole person and the whole field of interpersonal behaviour. This is analogous to the natural process by which all the branches; leaves, flowers, and fruit of a tree can be simultaneously nourished and enlivened by watering the root.

The Self can be directly experienced. Those who do experience it find it to be deeply peaceful, yet a reservoir of creativity, intelligence, and happiness that spills over into all phases of living.

Self-Correcting Mechanism of Checks & Balances

The human body is part of nature, as mentioned before a microcosm of the universe, and when it runs perfectly, as it was designed to run, one is in perfect health. It is trying to be perfectly healthy all the time, using its innate self-healing, self-regulating ability as it strives for a perfect homeostatic balance. But unfortunately we repeatedly interfere.

Nature has set us up with all the equipment we need to be perfectly healthy. Health is our natural state, and ill health is unnatural. Every day our systems are exposed to literally millions of bacteria, viruses, allergens, even carcinogens, and yet our immune system has the intelligence and skill to deal with all those invaders and keep us healthy. However, when stress, inadequate nutrition, or just fatigue weakens the immune system it results in ailments and disorders.

Ayurveda holds that specific disease conditions are symptoms of an underlying imbalance. It does not neglect relief of these symptoms, but its main focus is on the big picture: to restore balance and to help you lead a healthy lifestyle such that imbalances do not occur.

Living in health and balance is the key to a long life free from disease. Perhaps the most important lesson Ayurveda has to teach is that our health is up to us. Every day of our lives, every hour of every day, we can, and do, choose either health or illness. When we choose wisely, nature rewards us with health and happiness. When we persistently choose unwisely, nature, in her wisdom, eventually sets us straight: She makes us sick and gives us a chance to rest and rethink our choices.

Nirgundi
Lat: Vitex negundu
Malayalam: Karinochi
Useful part: Roots and leaves
Main Indications: cough, cold, inflammatory dis.

11

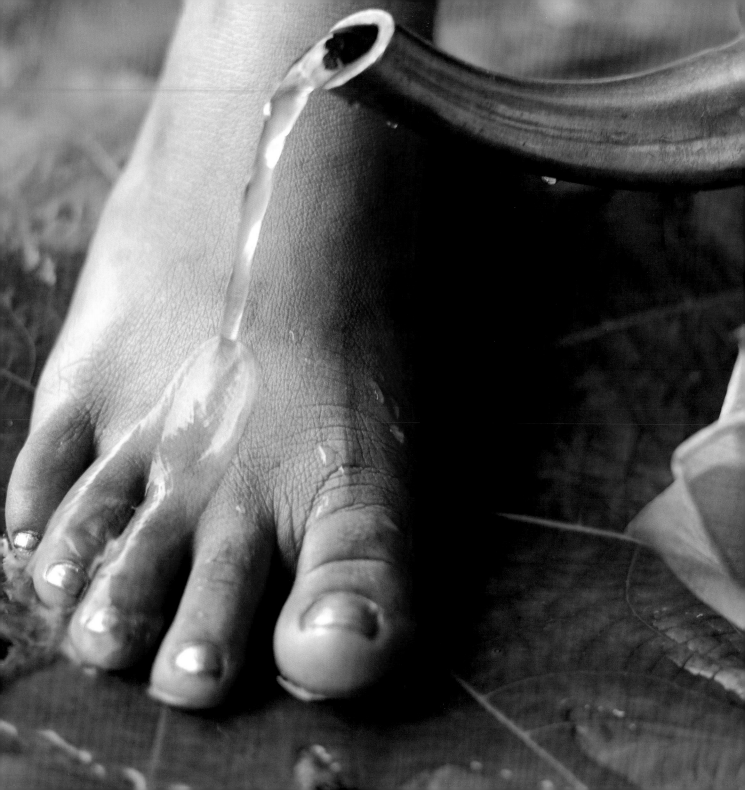

The Philosophy of Ayurveda

Ayurveda draws its concepts and theories from Hindu schools of philosophy such as Samkhya, Yoga and Nyaya. The fundamental doctrine of Ayurveda postulates that the five eternal elements of **Space, Air, Earth, Water** and **Fire** known as 'Panchamahabhoota' comprise the universe. The theory of Panchamahabhoota evolved in the post-Vedic period from 500 BC around the time that the Upanishads – the primary spiritual teachings of ancient India were written. Everything contained in the universe, including the human body is believed to be composed of these of Panchamahabhoota in varying compositions. The quality and nature of all matter, living and non-living is dependent relative to the variation in proportion of these elements. It is the divergence in the balances of these basic elements that lend distinct physical and chemical characteristics to all that is found in nature. The only additional feature that living things are credited with is '**Chaithanya;**' or spirit/soul.

Space is the place where everything happens. It is the field that is simultaneously the source of all matter and it is only distances that separate matter. The chief characteristic of space is sound. Here sound represents the entire spectrum of vibration.

Air is the gaseous form of matter that is both itinerant and dynamic. Within the body, air (oxygen) is the basis for all energy transfer reactions. It is a key element required for fire to burn. Air is the mixture of gases without form.

Earth represents the solid state of matter. It manifests stability, permanence, and rigidity. In our body, the parts such as bones, teeth, cells, and tissues are manifestations of the earth. Earth is considered a stable substance.

Water characterizes change and represents the liquid state. Water is necessary for the survival of all living things. A large part of the human body is made up of water. It is the movement of blood and other vital bodily fluids through our cells that generate energy, carrying away wastes, regulating temperature, sustain disease fighters, and carrying hormonal information from one area to another. Water is a substance without stability.

| SPACE | AIR | FIRE | WATER | EARTH |

Fire is the power to transform solids into liquids, to gas, and back again. In other words, it possesses the power to transform the state of any substance. Within our bodies, the fire or energy binds the atoms together. It also converts food to fat (stored energy) and muscle. Fire transforms food into energy. It creates the impulses of nervous reactions, our feelings, and even our thought processes. Fire is considered a form without substance.

Every substance in the universe is made up of these five substances. All substances can be classified according to their predominant element. For example, a mountain is predominantly made up of earth element while it also contains water, fire, air and ether. But these elements are very small in proportion to the earth element and hence a mountain is classified as earth.

Ayurveda defines a human being as an assembly of the Panchamahabhoota plus Chaithanya.

The Senses

The Panchamahabootha manifests in the functioning of the 5 basic senses of human beings. This permits a person to perceive the external environment in which he or she lives. They are also related, through the senses, to five actions expressing the functions of the sensory organs.

The basic senses and their relationship to the Panchamahabootha are given below:

Element	Senses	Organ	Action	Organ of Action
Space	Hearing	Ear	Speech	Tongue, vocal cords, mouth
Air	Touch	Skin	Holding	Hand
Earth	Smell	Nose	Excretion	Anus
Water	Taste	Tongue	Procreation	Genitals
Fire	Vision	Eye	Walking	Feet

Like and Unlike

Anything that enters our body (microcosm) can have three possible side effects. It can act as food that nourishes, it can act as medicine that balances and it can act as poison that harms the body. The five elements may exert one, two, or all three of these effects. The rule that governs the interaction between the environment and the organism is the Law of Like and Unlike. Like increases like while the unlike decreases like.

For example, when you sunbathe the body temperature goes up. Similarly, when you bathe in cold water, the body temperature goes down. Everything you experience, food, medicine, or poison, increases like parts of your microcosm and decreases those parts that are unlike it. Similarly, thought also enters your microcosm. Thought can be positive or negative and will influence your being. Good thoughts cheer us up. Bad thoughts poison us and decrease the feeling of well-being. Knowing what are good and bad for ourselves enable us to make informed choices in life. Right thoughts and attitudes actually provoke prosperity. Evil thoughts and bad deeds will result in the ultimate ruin of the microcosm.

The Tridosha Theory

The presence of Panchamahabhoota or the five eternal elements is apparent in the human body as subtle energies namely - 'Doshas;' which maintain and control the metabolic activities of the body, 'Dhatu;' the basic functional tissues that support bodily functions, 'Mala;' the metabolic by-products which are partly used in the body and partly excreted, 'Agni;' the representative of solar energy in living organisms and the catalytic agent for every kind of metabolism, and 'Triguna;' the three specific properties of the mind, which ensures the smooth functioning of the three Doshas, seven Dhatus and three Malas. The dynamic equilibrium of these elements upholds perfect health and imbalances if any leads to illness.

Dosha, as the term denotes, is that which maintains and controls the human body and is considered to be the most vital element. The effect of Panchamahabhoota manifest in Dosha as three fundamental humours namely: 'Vata', 'Pitta' and 'Kapha' - collectively known as the 'TRIDOSHA' in Sanskrit.

Doshas	Related Elements
Vata	Air and Ether
Pitta	Fire and Water / Fire
Kapha	Water and Earth

Tridosha (or the Three-Humour Theory) is the basis of Ayurveda. The space and air elements in combination form **Vata**, the fire and water elements constitute **Pitta** and earth & water elements form **Kapha**. The Tridosha govern the biological, physiological and pathological functions of the body, mind and consciousness. The Tridosha while not prevalent to the naked eye is perceived to be basic constituents and protective barriers of the human body in its normal physiological condition.

Vata Principle: Vata is considered to be the primary Dosha as it governs the right functioning of the other two. Main site of it is below the navel – in the urinary bladder, pelvic region, intestines, legs, thighs and bone. An imbalance in Vata results in lassitude of the limbs, tanning of the skin, shivering, gastric formations, constipation, insomnia, and weakness in bodily organs, giddiness and erratic speech. It also causes general weakness of the body, anaemia, respiratory malfunctions and lethargy. A proper balance of Vata ensures smooth breathing & bodily movement, quickness in comprehension, smooth excretion of metabolic wastes and general alertness.

Pitta Principle: Pitta is considered to be mainly present between the heart and the navel – in the navel itself, stomach and upper parts of the small intestines, sweat, lymph, blood, eyes and skin. Any imbalance in Pitta results in pale eyes, skin, stool and urine combined with an erratic in appetite. The body also experiences a burning sensation and sleeplessness is a typical symptom. The skin loses its natural lustre and there is often shivering of the body. A proper balance of Pitta results in good appetite, proper digestion, bodily warmth, keen eyesight, sharp memory, wisdom, courage and a glowing skin.

Kapha Principle: This is the phlegmatic principle and is considered to be present mainly in the chest, throat, head, joints, nose, fatty tissues, and tongue. Any imbalance in Kapha leads to sluggish digestion making the body feel stiff and lethargic. Often there is an excessive secretion of saliva, coldness in the joints, laboured breathing, cough and drowsiness. A proper balance in Kapha keeps the joints firm and maintains the right suppleness of the body.

Effect of Each Humour on Body

	VATA	PITTA	KAPHA
Function of the Doshas	Movement	Body heat	Stability
	Breathing	Temperature	Energy
	Natural Urges	Digestion	Lubrication
	Transformation of the tissues	Perception	Forgiveness
	Motor functions	Understanding	Greed
	Sensoryfunctions	Hunger	Attachment
	Ungroundedness	Thirst	Accumulation
	Secretions	Intelligence	Holding
	Excretions	Anger	Possessiveness
	FearEmptiness	Hate	
	Anxiety	Jealousy	
	Thoughts		
	Life force		
	Nerve impulses		
Manifests in living things as	The movement of Nerve impulses:	The quality of transformation. Pitta controls the enzymes that digest our food and the hormones that regulate our metabolism. Pitta transforms the chemical/electrical impulses in our mind to thoughts we can understand.	Cells that make up our organs and fluids, which nourish and protect them.
	Air		
	Blood		
	Food		
	Waste		
	Thought		

Effect of Each Humour on Body

	VATA	PITTA	KAPHA
Characteristics	Cold Light Irregular Mobile Rarefied Dry Rough	Hot Light Fluid Subtle Sharp Malodorous Soft Clear	Oily Cold Heavy Stable Dense Smooth
Too much of the Dosha forces can result in	Nerve irritation High blood pressure Gas Confusion.	Ulcers Hormonal imbalance Irritated skin (acne) Consuming emotions (anger)	Mucous build-up in the sinus and nasal passages, the lungs and colon. In the mind it creates rigidity, a fixation of thought, inflexibility.
Too little dosha force can result in	Nerve loss Congestion Constipation Thoughtlessness	Indigestion Inability to understand Sluggish metabolism	Experiences a dry respiratory tract burning stomach (due to lack of mucous, which protects from excess stomach acids) inability to concentrate.

Effect of Each Humour on Body			
	VATA	**PITTA**	**KAPHA**
Where found in a plant	Flowers and leaves (the parts which reach farthest into air and space)	Plant's essential oils, resins and sap	Roots (The roots are where water is stored. Roots also stay within the earth.)
Climatic influences	Dry climates or cold autumn winds increases Vata	Hot summers or hot climates will increase Pitta	Wet winters and damp climate add to Kapha.
Predominant during old age	As we get older, we "shrink and dry out".	Teens and Adults. During this stage, our hormone changes transforms us into adults	Childhood years. During this period, we grow or increase in substance of the body.

The Six Tastes

A balanced diet requires the understanding of the different food groups, nutrient values of the food and an understanding of the daily requirements of the food items. If a person consistently eats an unbalanced diet, his/her health will suffer from the deficiency of the nutrients to be obtained from the food or from the excess of the nutrients that is imbibed. For example, a diet that is high in saturated fat and red meat is known to cause hardening and blockage of the arteries ultimately resulting in coronary disorders. Due to ignorance about nutritive content of foods and the bodily requirements of nutrients amidst people of ancient India, Ayurveda advocates a simple and easy-to-follow dietary guidelines the six tastes. According to this system, all the important nutrients that we need for life, such as fats, proteins, carbohydrates, minerals, vitamins, etc. are contained in a meal that consist of all six tastes.

The six tastes are **sweet**, **sour**, **salty**, **bitter**, **pungent**, and **astringent**. Food that belongs to each of these tastes is given in the table. Any meal that contains food items from all these six tastes will be a balanced meal. It has all the nutrients for the proper functioning of the body and will balance all the doshas. This is a very simple system and easy to practice and follow.

Taste:	Sweet (Earth + Water)		
Property	Cooling		
Source / Example	Fruits with natural sugar such as peaches, sweet plums, grapes, melons, and oranges; vegetables such as sweet potatoes, carrots, and beets; milk, butter, and whole grains such as rice and wheat bread; herbs and spices such as basil, liquorice root, red cloves, peppermint, slippery Elm and fennel. Ayurveda recommends that you avoid highly processed sweets such as candy bars and sugar, which also contain additives, food colouring, and preservatives.		
Effect on Tridosha	Decreases Vata	Decreases Pitta	Increases Kapha
Actions	Sweet is the taste of pleasure. It makes us feel comforted and contented. It is one of the most important healing tools for debilitating weakness in Ayurveda. Nourishing and strengthening and promotes growth of all tissues, so is good for growing children, the elderly, and the weak or injured. Increases Ojas and prolongs life. Good for hair, skin and complexion, and for healing broken bones. Adds Wholesomeness to the Body. Increases Rasa, water and Ojas. Relieves thirst: Creates a burning sensation, Nourishes & soothes the body.		
Disorders	In excess, sweet taste promotes Kapha imbalances and disorders such as heaviness, laziness, and dullness, colds, obesity, excessive sleeping, loss of appetite, cough, diabetes, & abnormal growth of muscles.		

Taste:	Sour (Earth + Fire)		
Property	Heating		
Source / Example	Yoghurt, vinegar, Cheese, sour cream, Green Grapes, Lemon (and other Citrus fruits), Hibiscus, Rose Hips, Tamarind, Pickles, Miso (fermented soyabean paste) and in herbs such as Caraway, Coriander, and Cloves.		
Effect on Tridosha	Decreases Vata	Increases Pitta	Increases Kapha
Actions	Creates a feeling of adventurousness. Adds deliciousness to food. Stimulates Appetite & Sharpens the mind. Strengthens the sense organs. Causes secretions & salivation. Is Light, Hot & Unctuous. Good for the heart, digestion and assimilation. Helps dispel gas.		
Disorders	Increases thirst, Sensitivity of teeth, Closure of eyes, Liquefaction of Kapha, Toxicosis of blood, Edema, Ulceration, Heartburn & Acidity. You become weak and giddy. It also may cause itching and irritation, thirst, and blood toxicity.		

Taste:	Salty (Saline) (Water + Fire)		
Property	Heating		
Source / Example	Table salt, Sea Salt, Rock Salt, Kelp, seaweeds.		
Effect on Tridosha	Decreases Vata	Increases Pitta	Increases Kapha
Actions	A basic unit of electricity, salt helps retain moisture in Vata. Helps digestion. Acts as an Anti-spasmodic & Laxative. Promotes Salivation, Nullifies the Effect of all other Tastes. Retains Water. Heavy. Unctuous, Hot.		

Disorders	Excess salt can aggravate skin conditions, weaken the system, cause wrinkling of the skin and greying and falling out of hair. It promotes inflammatory skin diseases, gout, and other Pitta disorders. Disturbs Blood, Causes fainting & heating of the body. Causes peptic ulcer, rash, pimples & hypertension

Taste:	**Pungent** (Fire + Air)
Property	Heating
Source / Example	Onion, Radish, Chilli, Ginger, Garlic, Asafoetida, Cayenne Pepper, black pepper, mustard.

Effect on Tridosha	Increases Vata	Increases Pitta	Decreases Kapha

Actions	Stimulates appetite and improves digestion. Like salt and sour, pungent improves the taste of food. Gives mental clarity. Helps cure Kapha disorders such as obesity, sluggish digestion and excess water in the body. Improves circulation. Is germicidal, stops itching, facilitates sweating and elimination of Ama (toxic accumulations). Keeps the mouth clean. Purifies the blood, cures skin disease, helps to eliminate blood clots, cleanses the body. Light, Hot, Unctuous.
Disorders	Too much pungent taste can cause weakness, feeling of weariness, impurities, burning sensations in the body. Increases Heat, sweating, can cause a peptic ulcer, dizziness & unconsciousness.

Taste:	**Bitter** (Air + Earth)
Property	Cooling
Source / Example	Dandelion Root, Holy Thistle, Yellow Dock, Rhubarb, bitter melon, greens such as Romaine lettuce, spinach, and chard, Fresh Turmeric Root, Fenugreek, Gentian Root.

Effect on Tridosha	Increases Vata	Decreases Pitta	Decreases Kapha

Actions	Considered to be one of the most healing tastes for many kind of imbalances in the mind-body. Bitter foods and herbs are drying and cooling and create lightness. Promotes other tastes. Acts as an Antitoxic & Germicidal. Is an antidote for Fainting, Itching and Burning Sensations in the body. Relieves thirst. Good for reducing fevers. Promotes digestion. Cleansing of the blood and helps remove Ama in system.
Disorders	Too much bitterness can cause dehydration. It can also increase roughness, emaciation, dryness. Reduces bone marrow & semen. Can cause dizziness & Eventual unconsciousness.

Taste:	**Astringent** (Air + Earth)
Property	Cooling
Source / Example	Unripe Banana, Cranberries, Pomegranate, Myrrh, Goldenseal, Turmeric, Okra, Beans, Mace, Parsley, Saffron, Basil, and Alum.

Effect on Tridosha	Increases Vata	Decreases Pitta	Decreases Kapha

Actions	Astringent foods and herbs squeeze out water. Drying and firming, astringent taste stops diarrhoea, reduces sweating, and slows or stops bleeding. (Causes constriction of blood vessels, Coagulation of blood.) Anti-inflammatory. Promotes healing. Has a sedative action, but is constipating, dry, rough and cold.
Disorders	Excess astringent is weakening and causes premature aging. Its drying effect causes constipation and retention of gas. Promotes dry mouth. Promotes Vata disorders such as paralysis and spasms. Obstruction of speech. Too much astringent taste can adversely affect the heart.

PRAKRUTHI (or Constitutional Nature) of every individual is different and is predetermined at the time of conception based on the permutations and combinations of the Panchamahabhoota that manifest in the parental genes. But the combination of elements that govern the continuous psychopathological functioning of the body alters in response to the changes in the environment, food habits and daily routine.

Classification of Prakruthi

Three types of Prakruthi are generally recognised in Ayurveda.
These are:

Ekadosha

Dwidosha

Tridosha (sama)

A perfect balance of the three doshas is said to be sama prakruthi or balanced constitution. This is the ideal constitution as the balanced state of each dosha neutralizes any negative qualities and brings out the positive qualities permitting the person to lead a healthy lifestyle. A person with sama prakruthi will have maximum immunity and ability to balance and deal with any physical or psychological changes.

What is generally seen in nature is a predominance of a particular dosha, leading to Vata prakruthi, Pitta prakruthi or Kapha prakruthi. People with a predominance of any particular dosha are usually found to be more susceptible to ailments relating to those doshas. The most common prakruthi in

an individual is that which involves a combination of two doshas and as a result three more varieties of prakruthi have been recognised bringing the total to seven.

These are:

1. Vata, or 'wind-dominant type'
2. Pitta, or 'fire-dominant' type
3. Kapha, or 'phlegm-dominant' type
4. Vata - Pitta type
5. Vata - Kapha type
6. Pitta - Kapha type
7. Vata - Pitta - Kapha type
8. Pitta - Vata type
9. Kapha - Vata type
10. Kapha – Pitta type

Principal characteristics of each Prakruthi

The features of any prakruthi are dependent on the qualities of the particular dosha to which it relates. Each quality has a specific effect on the formation of characteristics.

Arka
Lat: Calotropis gigantea
Malayalam: Erukku
Useful part: all parts
Main Indications:
inflammatory dis., skin dis., Toxic conditions

Characteristics of a predominant Vata constitution:

- Creativity, mental quickness

- Highly imaginative

- Quick to learn and grasp new knowledge, but also quickly forget

- Sexually easily excitable but quickly satiated

- Slenderness; lightest of the three body types

- Talk and walk quickly

- Tendency toward cold hands and feet, discomfort in cold climates

- Excitable, lively, fun personality

- Changeable moods

- Irregular daily routine

- Variable appetite and digestive efficiency

- High energy in short bursts; tendency to tire easily and to over exert

- Full of joy and enthusiasm when in balance

- Respond to stress with fear, worry, and anxiety, especially when out of balance

- Tendency to act on impulse

- Often have racing, disjointed thoughts

- Generally have dry skin and dry hair and don't perspire much

Typical health problems include headaches, hypertension, dry coughs, sore throats, ear aches, anxiety, irregular heart rhythms, muscle spasms, lower back pain, constipation, abdominal gas, diarrhoea, nervous stomach, menstrual cramps, premature ejaculation and other sexual dysfunctions, arthritis. Most neurological disorders are related to Vata imbalance.

Physical Attributes

People of Vata constitution are generally physically underdeveloped Their chests are flat and their veins and muscle tendons are visible. The complexion is brown; the skin is cold, rough, dry and cracked.

Vata people generally are either too tall or too short, with thin frames that reveal prominent joints and bone-ends because of poor muscle development. The hair is curly and scanty, the eyelashes are thin and the eyes lustreless. The eyes may be sunken, small, dry, and active. The nails are rough and brittle. The shape of the nose is bent and turned-up.

Physiologically, the appetite and digestion are variable. Vata people loves sweet, sour and salty tastes and like hot drinks. The production of urine is scanty and the faeces are dry, hard and small in quantity. They have a tendency to perspire less than other constitutional types. Their sleep may be disturbed and they will sleep less than the other types. Their hands and feet are often cold. Psychologically, short memory but quick mental understanding characterizes them.

They will understand something immediately, but will soon forget it. They have little willpower, tend toward mental instability and possess little tolerance, confidence or boldness. Their reasoning power is weak and these people are nervous, fearful and afflicted by much anxiety.

Vata people tend to earn money quickly and also to spend it quickly. Thus, they tend to remain poor.

Characteristics of a predominant Pitta constitution

Here are some of the common characteristics of people who have a predominantly Pitta body type.

- Medium physique, strong, well-built
- Sharp mind, good concentration powers
- Orderly, focused
- Assertive, self-confident, and entrepreneurial at their best; aggressive, demanding, pushy when out of balance
- Competitive, enjoy challenges
- Passionate and romantic; sexually have more vigour and endurance than Vatas, but less than Kaphas
- Strong digestion, strong appetite; get irritated if they have to miss or wait for a meal
- Like to be in command
- When under stress, Pittas become irritated and angry
- Skin fair or reddish, often with freckles; sunburns easily
- Hair usually fine and straight, tending toward blond or red, typically turns grey early; tendency toward baldness or thinning hair
- Uncomfortable in sun or hot weather; heat makes them very tired
- Perspire a lot
- Others may find them stubborn, pushy, and opinionated
- Good public speakers; also capable of sharp, sarcastic, cutting speech
- Generally good management and leadership ability, but can become authoritarian
- Like to spend money, surround themselves with beautiful objects
- Subject to temper tantrums, impatience, and anger

Typical physical problems include rashes or inflammations of the skin, acne, boils, skin cancer, ulcers, heartburn, acidity and sensation of heat or intestines, insomnia, bloodshot or burning eyes and other vision problems, anaemia, jaundice.

Erandam
Latin: Ricinus communis
Malayalam: Avanakku
Useful parts: root, leaves,
oil of the seeds.
Main indication: constipation,
Rheumatism, sciatica etc.

Characteristics of Kapha Types

Here are some of the common characteristics of people who have a predominantly Kapha constitution.

- Easygoing, relaxed, slow-paced
- Affectionate and loving
- Forgiving, compassionate, non-judgemental nature stable and reliable; faithful
- Physically strong and with a sturdy, heavier build
- Have the most energy of all constitutions, but it is steady and enduring, not explosive
- Slow moving and graceful
- Slow speech, reflecting a deliberate thought process
- Slower to learn, but never forgets; outstanding long-term memory
- Soft hair and skin; tendency to have large "soft" eyes and a low, soft voice
- Prone to heavy, oppressive depressions
- Tend toward being overweight; may also suffer from sluggish digestion
- More self-sufficient, need less outward stimulation than do the other types A mild, gentle, and essentially undemanding approach to life
- Sexually Kaphas are the slowest to be aroused, but they also have the most endurance
- Excellent health, strong resistance to disease
- Slow to anger; strive to maintain harmony and peace in their surroundings
- Not easily upset and can be a point of stability for others
- Tend to be possessive and hold on to things, people, money; good savers. Don't like cold, damp weather.

Physical problems include colds and congestion, sinus headaches, respiratory problems including asthma and wheezing, hay fever, allergies, and arteriosclerosis or hardening of the arteries.

How to recognize the body type.

If one dosha is much higher than both others you are single dosha type (eg. Vata - 45, Pitta - 30, Kapha - 25). A single dosha type exhibits the characters of that particular type Prominently compared to the second higher dosha traits.

If two dosha have close scores and one very low then you are two doshas type. (eg: Vata - 20, Pitha - 42, Kapha - 48). You are Kapha Pitha.

Here your Kapha traits may dominate; but pitha traits are also prominent to a good extent. Three dosha type : If three dosha scores come almost equal you can be considered three dosha type. As this type is rare you have to double check for the confirmation.

To find out your body type you have to go through the following quiz and mark the most suitable for you. At the end count the score and see which is your constituition.

Vata

	Not suitable	Somewhat suitable	Most suitable
	1	**2**	**3**
I have a tall thin and poorly developed physique			
I have dark dull skin colour			
I hate cold, wind and sensitive to dryness.			
I have a variable and erratic appetite			
I am very quick in my actions and a fast walker.			
I have a poor, variable and weak immune system.			
I am enthusiastic and bubbly by nature			
I have a tendency for constipation and flatulence			
I tend to become anxious or worried easily and frequently.			
Decision making is difficult for me.			
I speak quickly and may be talkative.			
I have light sleep and tendency for sleeplessness.			
I am active by mind; also imaginative and some times restless.			
I get excited very easily.			
I learn quickly, but also forget fast.			
I like moving, travelling, plays. Jokes & stories.			
Total Vata score			

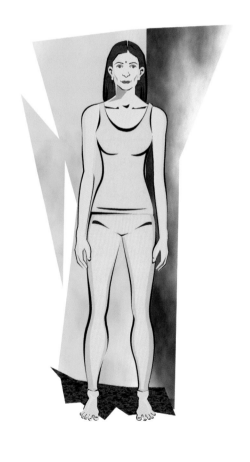

Pitta

	Not suitable 1	Somewhat suitable 2	Most suitable 3
I have medium, moderately developed physique.			
I have a red fair flushed complexion.			
I hate heat; dislike sun and fire.			
I have a sharp and strong appetite.			
I'm precise and orderly in my activities.			
I have a medium resistance and am prone to infections.			
I am intelligent, critical and penetrating.			
I am regular in my bowel habits and have a tendency for loose stools. than to constipation.			
I get angry quite easily, but quickly forget about it.			
I am strong minded and have a some what forceful manner.			
I am argumentative and convincing			
I get good sleep, may wakeup but fall asleep again.			
My friends consider me stubborn			
I become impatient very easily			
I like challenges and am determined			
I like cold foods and perspire easily.			
Total Pitta score			

Kapha

	Not suitable 1	Somewhat suitable 2	Most suitable 3
I have a big, stout, well developed physique			
I have a white, pale complexion.			
I dislike cold, damp atmosphere and like wind and sun.			
I can skip meals without any significant discomfort.			
I do things in a slow relaxed fashion and walk with measured steps.			
I have a strong immune system with consistent resistance.			
I am calm and not easily angered or excited.			
My bowel habit is moderate with solid stool with mucous.			
I have a slow, steady and dull mental nature.			
I eat slowly and am slow and methodical in actions.			
I am not talktive, slow and definite in speech			
I sleep deeply and have a tendency to over sleep			
I am calm content, attached and sentimental			
I put on weight easily and lose it more slowly.			
I learn slowly; but never forget.			
I like water, sailing, flowers, cosmetics and business.			

Total Kapha score

33

Signs of Vata Dosha Imbalance

There are a number of telltale signs of dosha imbalance. Some persons will get very angry. Some get depressed etc. Here is a summary of the signs of Vata imbalance:

- Worried
- Tired, yet can't relax, Fatigue, poor stamina
- Nervous, Can't concentrate
- Anxious, fearful
- Agitated mind
- Impatient, anxious or hyperactive
- Spaced out
- Self-defeating
- Shy, insecure, Restless
- Cannot make decisions
- Weight loss, under weight
- Insomnia; wake up at night and can't go back to sleep
- Generalized aches, sharp pains, Arthritis, stiff and painful joints
- Agitated movement
- Very sensitive to cold
- Nail biting
- Rough, flaky skin, Chapped lips
- Fainting spells
- Heart palpitations
- Constipation, Intestinal bloating, gas, Belching, hiccups
- Dry, sore throat, Dry eyes

Symptoms of Vata Aggravation

- Worried
- Tired, yet can't relax, Fatigue, poor stamina
- Nervous, Can't concentrate
- Anxious, fearful
- Agitated mind
- Impatient, Antsy or hyperactive
- Spaced out
- Self-defeating
- Shy, insecure, Restless
- Cannot make decisions
- Weight loss, under weight
- Insomnia; wake up at night and can't go back to sleep
- Generalized aches, sharp pains, Arthritis, stiff and painful joints
- Agitated movement
- Very sensitive to cold
- Nail biting
- Rough, flaky skin, Chapped lips
- Fainting spells
- Heart palpitations
- Constipation, Intestinal bloating, gas, Belching, hiccups
- Dry, sore throat, Dry eyes

In summary, if you are suffering from anxiety, worry, a tendency to overexertion, insomnia, chronic tiredness, mental and emotional depression, physical tension and other symptoms of stress, a weakened immune system, headaches, underweight, constipation, skin dryness, mental confusion, emotional conflict, inability to make decisions, impulsiveness, fast and disconnected speech, fantasy, illusions, and sensations of being light-hearted and removed from thoughts, feelings, or circumstances, then there is a very good sign that your Vata is aggravated. Follow the dietary guidelines given to balance Vata dosha.

Indications of balanced Vata influences are mental alertness and abundance of creative energy, good elimination of waste matters from the body, sound sleep, a strong immune system, enthusiasm, emotional balance, and orderly functioning of the body's systems.

Tips on Health & Wellness for Vata Persons

The Vathas find it very difficult to maintain regular habits, that is, to eat and sleep at regular times. But this is the most important thing for them to do. When Vata is out of balance this may feel almost impossible, but an effort to establish a regular routine is very important for all people with a Vata body type. Rest sufficiently, and choose foods, behaviours, personal relationships, and environmental circumstances that can be instrumental in balancing Vata characteristics. It is also important to regulate mental and physical impulses and to modify mental attitudes, emotional states, and behaviours in supportive ways.

Sweet, sour, and salty tastes decrease Vata influences, so include these tastes if Vata influences need to be diminished. Milk, wheat, rice, and some fruits and berries can provide sweet and sour tastes. Regular exercise should be relaxed and moderate. Hatha yoga practice in a meditative mood is good, as are walking, and swimming. Avoid strenuous, competitive, frantic activities. Whenever possible associate with people who are calm and purposeful and meditate every day for deep relaxation.

Symptoms of Pitta Aggravation:

- Angry, Irritable
- Hostile, Enraged, Destructive
- Impatient
- Critical of self and others
- Argumentative, Aggressive
- Bossy, controlling
- Frustrated, Wilful, Reckless
- Acidity, heartburn, Stomach ulcer
- Fitful sleep, Disturbing dreams
- Diarrhoea, Food allergies
- Bad breath, Sour body odour
- Very sensitive to heat, Hot flashes
- Skin rashes
- Boils
- Bloodshot eyes
- Acne
- Weakness due to low blood sugar
- Fevers, Night sweats

Physical Traits

These people are of medium height, are slender and body frame may be delicate. Their chests are not as flat as those of Vata people and they show a medium prominence of veins and muscle tendons. The bones are not as prominent as in the Vata individual. Muscle development is moderate.

The Pitta complexion may be coppery, yellowish, reddish or fair. The skin is soft, warm and less wrinkled than Vata skin. The hair is thin, silky, red or brownish and there is a tendency toward premature greying of hair and hair loss. The eyes may be grey, green or cooper-brown and sharp: the eyeballs will be of medium prominence. The nails are soft. The shape of the nose is sharp and the tip tends to be reddish.

Physiologically, these people have a strong metabolism, good digestion and resulting in strong appetites. The person of Pitta constitution usually takes large quantities of food and liquid. Pitta types have a natural craving for sweet, bitter and astringent tastes and enjoy cold drinks. Their sleep is of medium duration but uninterrupted. They produce a large volume of urine and the faeces are yellowish, liquid, soft and plentiful. There is a tendency toward excessive perspiring. The body temperature may run slightly high and hands and feet will tend to be warm. Pitta people do not tolerate sunlight, heat or hard work well.

Psychologically, Pitta people have a good power of comprehension; they are very intelligent and sharp and tend to be good orators. They have emotional tendencies toward hate, anger and jealousy. They are ambitious by nature and generally turn out to be leaders. Pitta people appreciate material prosperity and they tend to be moderately well off financially. They enjoy exhibiting their wealth and luxurious possessions.

When you experience symptoms such as, excessive body heat, digestive problems, a tendency to be hostile or angry and controlling, impatience, a tendency to exert excessive effort to achieve goals, vision difficulties, and being prone to make errors in judgement because of mental confusion or because passion or emotion blurs powers of intellectual discernment, there is a good possibility that you are suffering from Pitta imbalance. **Indications of balanced Pitta influences** are strong powers of digestion, vitality, goal-setting inclinations, good problem-solving skills, keen powers of intelligence, decisiveness, boldness and courage, and a bright complexion.

Aswagandha
Lat: Withania somnifera
Malayalam: Amukkuram
Useful part: Root
Main Indications: Insomnia

Tips on Health & Wellness for Pitta Persons

Pitta constitutions will be upset by alcohol and cigarettes, as well as by overwork, overexertion, and overheating. When out of balance, they are susceptible to feeling such negative emotions as hostility, hatred, intolerance, and jealousy. Therefore it is very important for Pithas to keep their cool both literally and figuratively and to lead a pure and moderate lifestyle. Choose foods, attitudes, behaviours, personal relationships, and environmental circumstances, which can be instrumental in balancing Pitta characteristics.

Because sweet, bitter, and astringent tastes decrease Pitta influences, include these in your food plan if Pitta characteristics are too pronounced. Complex carbohydrates, milk, and some fruits are sweet; some green, leafy vegetables are bitter; beans and some green vegetables are astringent.

Do things that cool the mind, emotions, and body. Avoid conflicts. Cultivate the virtues of honesty, morality, kindness, generosity, and self-control.

Physical Features

People of Kapha constitution have well-developed bodies. There is, however, a strong tendency for these individuals to carry excess weight. Their chests are expanded and broad. The veins and tendons of Kapha people are not obvious because of their thick skin and their muscle development is good. The bones are not prominent.

Their complexions are fair and bright. The skin is soft, lustrous and oily it is also cold and pale. The hair is thick, dark, soft and wavy. The eyes are dense and black or blue. The whites of the eye are generally very white, large and attractive.

Physiologically, Kapha people have regular appetites. Due to slow digestion, they tend to consume less food. They crave pungent, bitter and astringent foods. Stools are soft and may be pale in colour: evacuation is slow. Their perspiration is moderate. Sleep is sound and prolonged. There is a strong vital capacity evidenced by good stamina, and Kapha people are generally healthy, happy and peaceful.

Psychologically, they tend to be tolerant, calm, forgiving and loving: however, they also exhibit traits of greed, attachment, envy and possessiveness. Their comprehension is slow but definite : once they understand something, that knowledge is retained.

Kapha people tend to be wealthy. They earn money and are good at holding on to it.

Hreeberam
Lat: Andropogon muricatus
Malayalam: Iruveli
Useful part: whole plant.
Main Indications: fever

Signs of Kapha Aggravation

- Sluggish thinking, Dull thinking
- Groggy all day
- Apathetic, no desire
- Depressed, Sad, Sentimental
- Slow to comprehend, Slow to react
- Procrastinating, Lethargy
- Clingy, hanging on to people and ideas
- Greedy, Possessive, Materialistic
- Sleeping too much
- Very tired in the morning, hard to get out of bed
- Drowsy or groggy during the day
- Weight gain, obesity
- Mucus and congestion in the chest or throat
- Mucus and congestion in the nose or sinuses Nausea
- Diabetes
- Hay fever
- Pale, cool, clammy skin
- Oedema, water retention, Bloated feeling
- Sluggish digestion, food "just sits" in the stomach
- High cholesterol
- Aching joints or heavy limbs

When you experience symptoms such as nausea, lethargy, a feeling of heaviness, chills, looseness of the limbs, coughing, mucus discharges, breathing difficulties, and a tendency to sleep too much, you may be suffering from Kapha imbalance. Other symptoms can be inertia, congestion, stagnation, and circulation problems. There may be a tendency toward obesity. Boredom, laziness, and mental dullness are typical symptoms.

Indications of a balanced Kapha influence are physical strength, a strong immune system, serenity, mental resolve, rational thinking, ability to conserve and use personal resources, endurance, and adaptability.

Tips for Health and Wellness for Kapha Types

Kaphas are prone to lethargy, sluggishness, depression, and overweight, Kaphas need activity and stimulation. Daily exercise is more important for them than for any other type. Getting out of the house and actively seeking new experiences is also valuable. Be receptive to useful change, renounce impediments to progress, be intentional in implementing life-enhancing actions, and choose foods, mental attitudes, behaviours, exercise routines, and relationships and environmental circumstances which can be instrumental in balancing Kapha characteristics.

Pungent, bitter, and astringent tastes decrease Kapha influences. Black pepper, ginger, cumin, chilli, and some other spices provide the pungent taste; some green leafy vegetables provide bitter taste; and some green vegetables and beans provide the astringent taste. Note that the taste that decreases a dosha usually increases one or both of the other two. For general purposes, mildly increase the proportion of foods that are helpful while somewhat decreasing the proportions of others - having a sampling of all six tastes at your major meal.

Meditation can be more intensive for Kapha constitutions than for Vata or Pitta constitutions. Schedule time every day for prayer and meditation.

Diet for each Dosha (Food)
Recommended Diet for Vata Type

These guidelines can be used for Vata mind-body constitutions, to maintain dosha balance, and to restore balance if necessary, regardless of the basic constitution. Vata influences the movement of thoughts, feelings, prana flows, nerve impulses, and fluids in the body.

- Warm food, moderately heavy textures, added butter and fat.
- Salt, sour, and sweet tastes; Soothing and satisfying foods.
- All soothing foods are good for settling disturbed Vata. Use foods such as: warm milk, cream, butter, warm soups, stews, hot cereals, and fresh baked bread. Since Vata is a cold dry dosha, warm, nourishing foods such as these are good for stabilizing Vata. On the other hand cold foods such as cold salads, iced drinks, raw vegetables and greens are not very good for persons with Vata imbalance.
- Breakfast is highly recommended. Use hot cereals such as cream of rice or wheat or any other breakfast that is warm, milky, and sweet.
- Take a hot or herbal tea with snacks in the late afternoon. Avoid drinks with high caffeine as it disturbs Vata.
- Use spicy foods such as spicy Mexican or Indian foods that are cooked in oil.
- Use warm moist foods such as cooked grains and cereals, bowl of hot oatmeal or cup of steaming vegetable soup.
- Warm milk is recommended. You can add a little sugar or honey to it if you prefer. Avoid eating candies as it disturbs Vata.
- Opt for salted nuts that are heavy and oily as opposed to dry salty snacks.
- All sweet fruits are OK for Vata. Avoid unripe fruits as they are astringent
- Take warm or hot water instead of ice water and drinks.

Summary: Breakfast is usually desirable. Hot foods and sweet and sour tastes. Reduce dry foods and bitter tastes. Warm or hot water and drinks. Raw nuts and nut butters. Spices: cinnamon, cardamom, cumin, ginger, cloves in moderation.

Food favourable and unfavourable for Vata Type

Favourable	Reduce or avoid
A Fruits Oranges,Bananas, coconut, Grapes, Mangoes pappaya, Pineapple, plums, peach, Cherries, berries, dates, Figs sweet, well ripened fruits in general.	Apple (uncooked), melons cranberries, unripe fruits Dry friuts in general
B Vegetables Carrots, Cucumber, Ashgourd, Beat root Radish, Onions and Garlic (cooked), chillies sweet potatoes, Corn, Artichoke,	Cauliflower, sprouts, cucumber, celery, , tomato, asparagus, spinach, mushrooms
C Grains Oats, Wheat, brown rice, Basmati rice	Corn, Rye, Barley, millet, buckwheat
D Beans Mungbeans, Tofu (in moderation)	All beans except mung
E Nuts & Seeds All nuts and seeds are good and almond the best.	
F Dairy All dairy products acceptable except ice cream	
G Animal Products Chicken, Turkey, Seafoods in general, Buttermilk, ghee	Red meat
H Oils & Sweeteners Almost all oils and sweetness are good	Safflower, corn, soy, margarine, white sugar
I Spices Almost all spices in moderation is good	Large amounts of any spices is noot good Minimize bitter and astringent spices such as coriender seeds, fenugreek, saffron, turmeric and parsley

Recommended Diet for Pitta Type

These guidelines can be used for Pitta mind-body constitutions, to maintain dosha balance and to restore balance if necessary regardless of the basic constitution. Pitta influences digestion and metabolism, body temperature, and biological transformations.

- Cool or warm but not steaming hot foods
- Bitter, sweet, and astringent tastes
- As far as practical use less butter and added fat. Consume food with moderately heavy textures.
- Since Pithas have strong efficient digestion, they can generally eat just about everything. Most Pithas get into trouble by continued use of too much salt, overuse of sour and spicy food and overeating.
- Take cool, refreshing food in summer. Reduce the consumption of salt, oil, and spices, all of which are "heating" to the body. Salads are good, so is milk and ice cream.
- Avoid pickles, yoghurt, sour cream, and cheese. Avoid vinegar in salad dressing; use lemon juice instead. Alcoholic and fermented foods should be avoided. Their sour Rasa aggravates Pitta. Coffee is also Pitta aggravating due to the acid in coffee.

Herb tea is good. Prefer mint, liquorice root or other Pitta pacifying tea.

- Breakfast: Cold cereals, cinnamon toast, and apple tea is a good breakfast for Pitta. Avoid coffee, orange juice and doughnuts - they aggravate Pitta.
- The vegetarian foods are the best for Pitta. Consuming red meat tends to heat the body from the fat. Consume abundant amounts of milk, grains and vegetables. Avoid oily, hot, salty, and heavy foods such as fried food. Instead consume starchy foods such as vegetables, grains and beans. Avoid the tendency to overeat under stress.
- Avoid processed and fast foods, as they tend to be heavy on salt and sour tastes. Japanese and Chinese foods are good alternatives. Avoid spicy food such as is found in Mexican restaurants.
- To bring down aggravated Pitta, take two teaspoons of ghee (clarified butter) in a glass of warm milk. Refrain from taking ghee for persons with high cholesterol levels.

In summer, avoid egg yolks, nuts, hot spices, honey, and hot drinks. Cool foods and drinks are better. Add sweet, bitter, and astringent tastes. Reduce use of sour tastes. Spices: black pepper, coriander, and cardamom.

Food favourable and unfavourable for Pitta Type

Favourable

A Fruits

Apple, orange, mango, plums, pears,cranberry grapes, pomegranates, melons, coconut, figs (all should be ripe & sweet)

B Vegetables

Cauliflower, Cucumber,Lettuce, asparagus, Potatoes, Parsley, bell pepper, corn, cabbage, Broccoli, Mushrooms, green beans, peas, Okra brussel sprouts, celery.

C Grains

Wheat, Basmati rice, white rice, barley, Oats

D Beans

Kidney beans, Soya & soyaproducts, Mung beans, peas (split) chick peas

E Nuts & seeds

Coconut & Sunflower

F Dairy

Milk, Cheese, cream, butter, Ghee (Clarified butter)

G Animal products

Chicken or turkey (white meat), egg white

H Oils & sweeteners

Coconut, Soya, sunflower all sweetness are good

I Spices

Cardamom, turmeric, mint,cumin, fennel, coriander, Generaly sweet, bitter and astringent once in small amounts

Reduce or avoid

Lemons,limes bananas, peaches, apricots, Papaya, strawberry, grape fruits, cherries berries

Onions (cooked), Carrot, beets, spinach, eggplant, radish, turnip, tomatoes, Chillies Onion (red)

Corn, rye, buck wheat, brown rice

Lentils & Peanuts

all except coconut & sunflower

Salted cheese, buttermilk,yogurt, sour creams

Red meat, pork, fish, egg yolk, beef, shell fish

Sesame, safflower, almond, corn, peanut Honey and molasses

Only minimal amount of mustard, salt & Vinegar

Recommended Diet for Kapha Type :

These guidelines can be used for Kapha mind-body constitutions, to maintain dosha balance, and to restore balance if necessary, regardless of the basic constitution. Kapha influences the heavy, moist aspects of the body. The type of food that balances Kapha is:

- Warm, light food, Dry food, cooked without much water, minimum of butter, oil and sugar, Stimulating foods with pungent, bitter, and astringent tastes.
- Kaphas need to watch the consumption of too much sweet foods or fatty foods. Keep an eye on the salt consumption also, which tend to result in fluid retention in Kaphas.
- Light meals are to be favoured such as light breakfast and dinner.
- Avoid deep fried foods. Eat lightly cooked foods or raw fruits and vegetables. Eat spicy, bitter and astringent foods. Do not overeat – a typical Kapha tendency.
- Select hot food over cold food whenever feasible. Dry cooking methods such as baking, broiling, grilling, or sautéing are recommended over moist cooking such as steaming, boiling or poaching.
- As appetizers eat bitter or pungent foods instead of salty or sour. Foods such as romaine lettuce, endive, or tonic water are good to stimulate your appetite.
- Take ginger tea or a pinch of ginger to stimulate appetite. Other preferred spices are cumin, fenugreek, sesame seed and turmeric.
- Any food that is spicy is good for Kaphas such as very hot Mexican or Indian food, especially in winter.
- Foods that are good for Kapha breakfast are hot-spiced cider, buckwheat pancakes with apple butter, corn muffins, and bitter cocoa made with skim milk and a touch of honey. Avoid cold cereals, cold juice or milk, and sugary pastries. Bacon and sausage aggravates Kapha due to their salt and oil.
- To pep you up in the morning, take honey, boiled and coled water, lemon juice and ginger. Try hot ginger tea. Try skipping a meal or two and try to sustain oneself on a spoonful of honey in water instead.
- Kaphas have a sweet tooth. So, cutting down on sugar is difficult for many of them. Reducing sugar intake recommended. Use honey instead. Avoid taking more than a spoonful of honey a day.
- Splurge on fresh fruits, vegetables and salads.

A late Breakfast is favourable. Avoid sugar, fats, dairy products, and salt. Ghee and oils should be consumed only in small amounts. Choose light, dry foods. The main meal should be at the middle of the day, and only a light, dry meal in the evening. Avoid cold foods and drinks. Reduce use of sweet, sour, and salty tastes. Pungent, astringent, and bitter tastes are all right. All spices are permissible.

Food favourable and unfavourable for Kapha Type

Favourable

Reduce or avoid

A **Fruits**
Apple, pomegranate, cranberries and dry fruits in general

bananas, coconut, dates, mangoes, melons Oranges, Papayas, peaches, Pears, Plums figs, pineapple, grapes, grapefruits

B **Vegetables**
Generally all including beets,broccoli, brussels sprouts, Carrot, Cabbage, cauliflower, celery, chillies, garlic, leafy green vegetable, lettuce mushrooms, onions, peans, peppers, potatoes, spinach

sweet and juicy vegetables such as cucumbers, tomatoes, sweetpotates, squash, okra, Zucchini

C **Grains**
barly, corn, buckwheat, rye, dry or popped grains in general

basmati rice, brown rice, oats, wheat, white rice

D **Beans**
all legumes are favourable

Tofu, chick & kidney beans

C **Nuts & Seeds**
Sunflower and   pumpkin seeds

all except sunflower & pumpkin

F **Dairy**
Goat's milk, soyamilk & butter milk

all except goat's, soya & buttermilk

G **Animal products**
Chicken, Turkey and, shrimp

Red meat, eggs & seafood in general

H **Oils & sweeteners**
Corn, mustard, safflower, sunflower, almond Honey is the only favourable sweetener

all oil except these
no sweeteners except honey

I **Spices**
all spices are good. Ginger is the best.

Salt.

Key Ayurvedic Concepts

Digestion - The Key to Good Health

According to Ayurveda, digestion is the basis of health. Good digestion nourishes the body. Eating the proper food will make a big difference in your well-being. There are two aspects to the food and nutrition in Ayurveda. One is the physical food you eat, digest, and assimilate. In this process, the organs of your digestive system have a big role. The second aspect of it is what you consume through your mind-body. What you see, hear, taste, smell, feel, and think are all-important for your well-being and impact your health considerably. For example, stress plays a key role in the health. Ayurveda had recognized the importance of the environment in the total health. Remember, everything in your environment is composed of doshas that interact with your own doshas. You are affected by everything else that goes on in this universe, as you are part and parcel of this cosmos. Thus we have the "big picture" or "holistic outlook" in Ayurveda.

Agni: Your Digestive Fire

Agni in Sanskrit means fire. In Ayurveda, Agni is the digestive and metabolic "fire" produced by the doshas that grabs the essence of nourishment from food, feelings, and thoughts and transforms it into a form your body can use. Agni helps various tissues of the body produce secretions, metabolic reactions, and other processes needed to create energy and maintain and repair the body. Agni is also part of the immune system since its heat destroys harmful organisms and toxins. The activity of Agni varies throughout the day and maintaining the strength and natural ebb and flow of your digestive fires is needed for good digestion, good immune function, and resistance to disease. Agni is needed to form Ojas.

Ojas: The Substance that Maintains Life

Ojas is the by-product of a healthy, efficient, contented physiology. It is the "juice" that remains after food has been properly digested and assimilated. When you are producing Ojas, it means all your organs have integrated vitality and you are receiving the nourishment your mind and body need. Your whole being hums with good vibrations because you are producing and feeling bliss, not pain. However, when your agni isn't working properly, you don't produce Ojas. Instead food, thoughts, and feelings turn into Ama. Ojas is the subtle glue that cements the body, mind and spirit together, integrating them into a functioning individual.

Tulasi
Lat: Oscimum sanctum
Malayalam: Tulasi
Useful part: Whole plant
Main Indications: Common cold, Skin diseases, Allergy, Toxins, Respiratory disorders.

Ama - Toxins

Ama originates from improperly digested toxic particles that clog the channels in your body. Some of these channels are physical and include the intestines, lymphatic system, arteries and veins, capillaries, and genitourinary tract. Others are non-physical channels called nadees meaning river or stream, through which your energy flows. Ama toxicity accumulates wherever there is a weakness in the body, and this will result in disease. Ayurveda offers ways you can cleanse the body of Ama such as Panchakarma. However, it's best to prevent it from forming in the first place. The symptoms such as coating on the tongue or feeling tired all the time are signs of Ama.

Malas: Waste Products

Malas are the waste products of your body and include urine, faeces, mucus, and sweat. Eliminating waste is crucial to good health, but dosha imbalances stifle the flow of the malas, creating a toxic internal environment. If you are not eliminating malas, it means you are accumulating Ama somewhere in your system and you may have to undergo Ayurvedic cleansing to get rid of these toxins from your body.

Prana: The Life Force

Another key concept in Ayurveda is the life force that enters the body at birth, travels through all the parts of the body until it leaves at the moment of death. This life force is called prana. Prana strings body, mind, and spirit together like beads on a strand. Prana is the force necessary to keep the living beings alive.

Prana gets its nutrition through:

- The lungs that absorb the essence found in the air.
- The colon absorbs the Prana found in well-digested food.

Thus the lungs and the large intestine are closely connected in Ayurveda. They both supply Prana. For example, a few minutes of slow, deep breathing can reduce the hunger. Ayurveda is concerned with nourishing both the body as well as the mind.

Nimba
Lat: Azadirachta indica
Malayalam: Aryaveppu
Useful part: Leaves, Bark, Root bark, Oil.
Main Indications: Allergy, Skin diseases,
As a blood purifier.

The Concept of Prakruthi and Vikruthi

According to Ayurveda, your basic constitution is determined at the time of conception. This constitution is called Prakruthi. The term Prakruthi is a Sanskrit word that means, "nature," "creativity," or "genesis." One of the very important concepts of Ayurveda is that one's basic constitution is fixed and remains unchanged throughout one's lifetime. The combination of Vata, Pitta, and Kapha present in an individual at the time of conception is remains constant. This is your very own stamp of individuality. People may have varying combinations of Vata, Pitta and Kapha as their basic constitution or Prakruthi. This is how Ayurveda can explain the subtle differences between individuals and explains why everyone is unique and that two persons can react very differently when exposed to identical stimuli. Your Prakruthi is as unique to you just as your fingerprints and DNA.

Ideally, your constitution remains fixed throughout your life. Unfortunately, this is not the case. Every person is subjected to the constant interaction with his or her environment, which will affect the person's constitution at any time. The body will try to maintain a dynamic equilibrium or balance with the environment. Your current condition is called your Vikruthi. Although it reflects your ability to adjust to life's influences and is always changing, it should match your Prakruthi, or inborn constitution, as closely as possible. If the current proportion of your doshas differs significantly from your constitutional proportion, it indicates imbalances, which in turn can lead to illness. Farther your Vikruthi is from your Prakruthi, more ill you are. Ayurveda teaches that your Vikruthi can be changed by means of diet and meditation so as to approach your Prakruthi or the state where you have perfect health.

Bhringaraja
Lat: Eclipta alba
Malayalam: Kayyonni
Useful part: Whole plant
Main Indications:Liver diseases,
Improve hair growth.

Kandakari
Lat: Solanum xanthocarpam
Malayalam: Kandakarichunda
Useful part: roots and fruits.
Main Indications: Respiratory dis, Alopacea

The concept of Prakruthi and Vikruthi can be illustrated by reference to our body temperature. When healthy, we maintain an average body temperature of about 98 degrees. Although there are slight variations in bodily temperature from individual to individual, the difference is negligible in a healthy person. When we go outside on a winter day, our body temperature may go down slightly; but will pick right back up to the normal if we are healthy. Similarly, jogging on a hot day can temporarily raise our body temperature. When we are sick, or catch a cold, our body temperature will go up.

This indicates that we are sick or outside our normal base condition. We may take medicine to bring the body temperature back to the normal range. In analogy to Ayurveda, our present temperature may be considered as Vikruthi and the difference between the Prakruthi (our normal temperature) and Vikruthi (our present temperature) can determine whether any medical intervention is required. Just like an allopathic doctor will take your temperature and blood pressure routinely as the first step in diagnosing your condition, Ayurvedic practitioners will determine your Prakruthi and Vikruthi as the first step in diagnosing your condition.

Hence prior to embarking on a journey to perfect health and longevity, it is important that you understand your Prakruthi and Vikruthi and determine how far separated these are. Armed with this knowledge, we can map a treatment strategy. This is the basic premise of Ayurveda.

Padmakam
Lat: Cesalpinia sappan
Malayalam: Patimukham
Useful part: Wood
Main Indications:Diuretic,
Blood purifier.

Sankhupushpi
Lat: Clitoria ternatea
Malayalam: Sankhupushpam
Useful part: roots and flowers
Main Indications: Insomnia, Mental disorders, improves intellect.

Dronapushpi
Lat: Lucas aspera
Malayalam: Tumpa
Useful part: Whole plant
Main Indications:Gynaecological problems, Fever, Toxins.

Treatment in Ayurveda

In the Ayurvedic system of medicine, identifying body types is of profound importance. There are various time-tested methods of identifying body types and it is not too difficult for an Ayurvedic expert to do so fairly quickly. Life-styles will need to be adjusted according to body type so as to resist diseases and maintain good health. Physical and mental co-operation of the patient to make necessary changes in his/her life style and food habits also are essential to attain the natural dynamic balance of the dosha and once that balance is attained the ailment disappears.

There are primarily three methods of diagnosis in Ayurveda.

1. Darsana Pareeksha or visual inspection of the patient.

2. Prasna Pareeksha or specific questioning of the patient.

3. Sparsana Pareeksha or physical examination.

Ayurveda gives special emphasis to prevention of disease. Signs and symptoms by which we can foresee an illness are well described in the texts so that we can take necessary steps to avoid it or lessen it's potency. Moreover, it teaches us to lead healthy lives devoid of ailments in any climate maintaining perfect health effectively. Strict followers of Ayurveda lead an enviable and enthusiastic life in tune with nature.

Treatment Types

The treatment types in Ayurveda can be classified mainly into two: 'Shamana Chikitsa' and 'Sodhana Chikitsa'

a, 'Shamana Chikitsa' (Alleviating Therapy)

Shamana Chikitsa is the pacifying way of treatment in less vitiation. Oral therapy and less hard-line external means are applied to correct the imbalances of the elements. In this therapy, unlike in Sodhana Chikitsa, restoration of normalcy is without elimination of any substances.

b, Sodhana Chikitsa (Purification Therapy)

As a result of constant metabolic activity a large amount of toxic bi-products accumulate in the human body most of which are eliminated naturally. However, some of this waste tends to get stuck in the various tissues of the body thus vitiating the dynamic equilibrium of the basic elements and causing disorders. Purification of these toxic wastes is the underlying principle of this therapy.

Dharturam
Lat: Datura stramonium
Malayalam: Ummam
Useful part: leaves and fruits
Main Indications: Bronchial asthma
and inflammatory diseases.

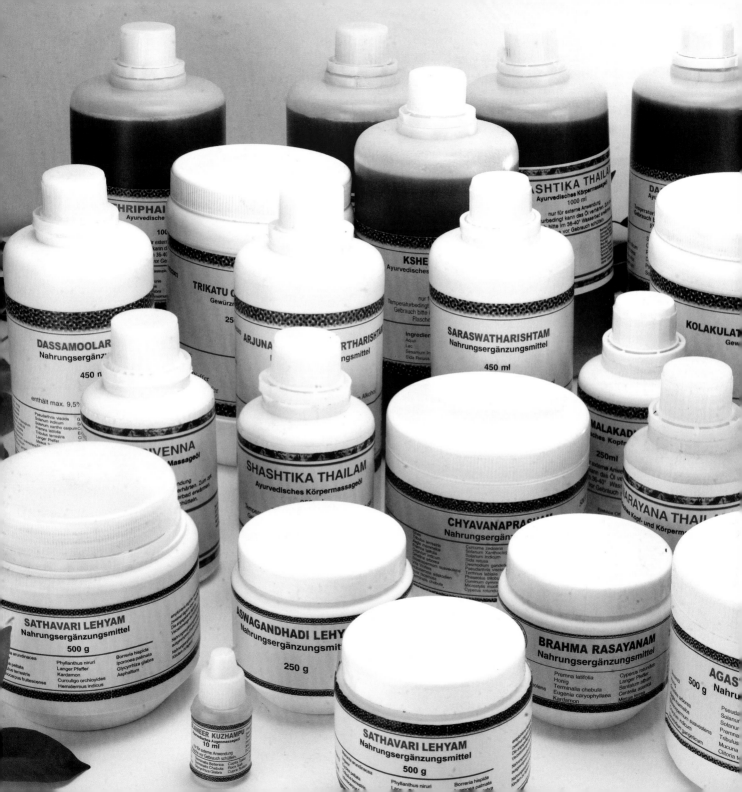

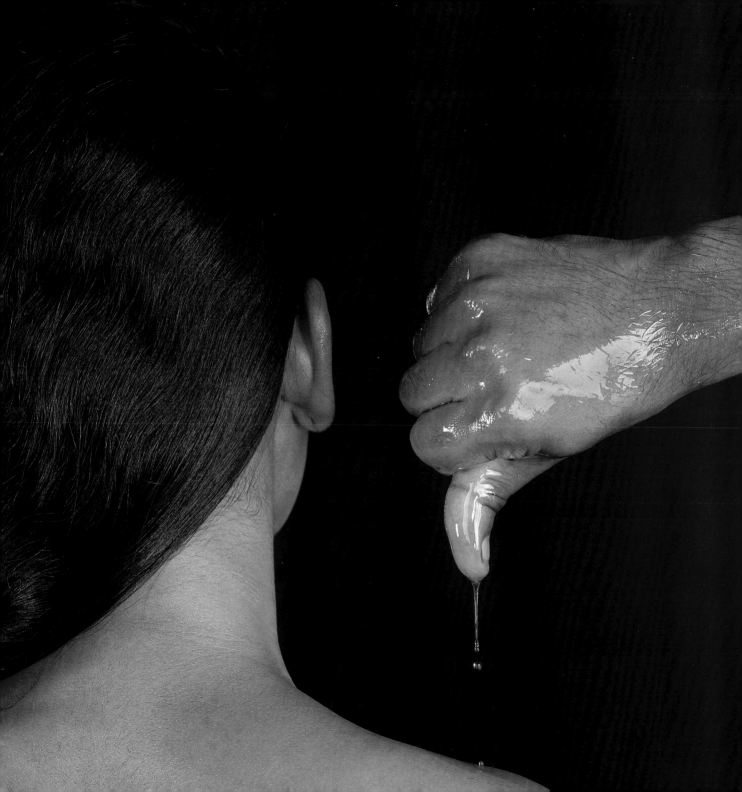

Panchakarma

Panchakarma is a Sanskrit word that means "five actions" or "five treatments." This is a process used to clean the body of toxic materials left by disease and poor nutrition. Ayurveda says that imbalanced doshas create waste matter. This waste matter is called Ama in Ayurveda. Ama is a foul-smelling, sticky, noxious substance that needs to be evacuated from the body as thoroughly as possible.

Panchakarma helps eliminate the excess doshas and/or imbalances in the doshas along with Ama out of your system by means of the body waste evacuation channels such as sweat glands, urinary tract, intestines, etcetera. Panchakarma is, thus, a balancing operation. Ayurveda recommends Panchakarma as a seasonal treatment for fine-tuning your body, mind and soul.

Steps in Panchakarma

Panchakarma is a five-fold therapy that is highly personalized based on the needs of the individual depending on the body type, dosha imbalances etcetera. Usually, only parts of the five therapies are needed.

Purwakarma

This breaks down into two types of preparatory treatment: "Snehana" and "Swedana."

Snehana involves internal an external oleation. Internal oleation is drinking of oil, clarified butter etc. and external oleation is massaging herbal oils onto the body. Oleation makes the body unctuous and improves the flow or humors by liquefying them and it dissolves the toxin also. Blended oils treat specific disorders such as stress, anxiety, insomnia, arthritis, or circulatory problems. Oils can also be massaged into the scalp for depression, insomnia, and memory problems. Snehana can sometimes involve lying in an oil bath, which is thought to be even more effective for you to absorb the herbal oils' properties.

Swedana means sweating. It is done after the oil treatment; some times on a separate day. Steam baths encourage the elimination of toxins and together with the oil treatments, they make the detoxification more effective.

Pretreatment

Prior to starting Panchakarma, oiling and heating of the patient is done to bring the excess doshas from the limbs to their proper reservoirs in the digestive tract, from which they can be expelled. The doshas are then excited by a procedure called utkleshana, a therapy that makes the excess dosha anxious to leave the body. One to three nights prior to the start of Vamana, the patient is asked to drink one cup of oil two to three times a day until the stool becomes oily, or he feels nauseated (This treatment is called oleation or snehana). Kaphagenic diet is given to aggravate Kapha. On the morning of the Panchakarma, kapha aggravating foods such as basmati rice and yogurt with salt is given to further aggravate the kapha. Oil massage and fomentation are administered on the night before the day of Vamana. The application of the heat to the chest and back will liquefy kapha.

Therapeutic vomiting or Vamana

This treatment is used when there is congestion in the lungs causing repeated attacks of bronchitis, cough, cold or asthma. The objective of the therapy is to induce vomiting to get rid of the mucus causing excess kapha. A drink consisting of licorice and honey, or calamus root tea is given to the patient. (Other substances used include salt, and cardamom) Rubbing on the tongue induces vomiting and it is usually induced 4 to 8 times depending on the prakruthi of the patient.

After vomiting the patient generally feels very comfortable; most of the congestion, wheezing and breathlessness will disappear along with the clearing of the sinus.

Therapeutic vomiting is used for cough, cold, symptoms of asthma, fever, nausea, loss of appetite, anaemia, poisoning, skin diseases, diabetes, lymphatic obstruction, chronic indigestion, oedema,, epilepsy (between attacks), chronic sinus problems, and for repeated attacks of tonsillitis.

Purgation Therapy or Vireka, Virechan; herbal laxative therapy

Virechan is the cleansing of the pitta and the purification of the blood toxins. Generally, it is administered three days after the Vamana treatment. If Vamana therapy is not needed, Virechan can be administered directly. Virechan cleanses the sweat glands, small intestine, colon, kidneys, stomach, liver, and spleen. A number of fine herbs are used as a laxative. These include senna, prune, bran, flaxseed husk, dandelion root, psyllium seed, cow's milk, salt, castor oil, raisins and mango juice. When taking these laxatives, it is important to adhere to restricted diet. Vireka is used for treatment of skin diseases, chronic fever, piles, abdominal tumors, worms, gout, jaundice, gastrointestinal problems, constipation, and irritable bowel syndrome.

Enema or Vasti

Medicated enemas are used for various specific reasons. In general, this treatment is used to flush the loosened doshas out through the intestinal tract. There are over 100 specific enemas listed in Ayurveda. Vasti involves introducing medicinal substances such as sesame oil, calamus oil, or other herbal decoctions in a liquid medium into the rectum. Vasti is especially good for vata disorders. It alleviates constipation, distension, chronic fever, the common cold, sexual disorders, kidney stones, heart pain, vomiting, backache, neck pain and hyper acidity. Such vata disorders as sciatica, arthritis, rheumatism, and gout can also be treated by Vasti.

There are about 80 vata related disorders in Ayurveda. About 80 percent of them can be treated with medicated enemas. Since vata is mainly located in the colon and bones, the medication is administered rectally.

Type of Enemas:
- Oil Enema or Anuvasana Vasti - 240 ml of medicated oil or ghee.
- Decoction enema or Nirooha Vasti (Herbal enema) Various combinations of decoction oil etc are prescribed.
- Nutrition Enema is another kind of decoction enema used for rejuvenation.

Enema should not be given to persons suffering from chronic indigestion, bleeding from rectum, cough, breathlessness, diarrhoea, diabetes, severe anaemia, to aged or to children under 7. Don't give decoction enemas to people suffering from acute fever, diarrhoea, cold, paralysis, heart pain, or severe pain in the abdomen.

Bloodletting or Rakta Moksha

Bloodletting is used to eliminate toxins that are absorbed into the bloodstream through the gastrointestinal tract. This process purifies the blood. It is used for disorders such as repeated attacks of skin disorders such as psoriasis, rash, eczema, acne, scabies, leucoderma, chronic itching, and hives. It was also found effective for enlarged liver and spleen, and for gout.

Bloodletting, which should only be administered by a qualified physician, is useful to relieve several pitta disorders such as acne and rash. If administered properly, it stimulates the antitoxic substances in the blood stream, thus developing the immune mechanism in the blood system.

Do not administer blood letting in cases of anaemia, oedema, and weakness or to very old and very young persons.

After detoxification the practitioner may prescribe herbal or mineral remedies to correct imbalances in the doshas. These have the necessary medicinal qualities to stimulate agni and restore balance in the doshas. They are not prescribed to eradicate disease because the disease is just a symptom of dosha imbalance.

Herbal remedies are usually prescribed in liquid form or as dried herbs, although they can also come as powder or tablets. The ingredients are pre-prepared, but the blends are prescribed individually. Each ingredient is classified by the effect it has on lowering or increasing levels of the doshas.

Most Ayurvedic practitioners will also advise you on lifestyle, food and exercise. There is no single healthy diet in Ayurveda, just a diet that is suitable for you. It is important to follow a diet most suitable for your body constitution and the practitioner may prepare a special diet plan for you to adhere to. Exercise, such as yoga, is also individually prescribed.

Nasal Administration or Nasyam, a herbal inhalation therapy

Nasal medication or sternutation is otherwise called 'Sirovirechana'. It benefits all the three humours and especially in 'vata' and 'kapha' aggravations. The excess humor accumulated in the head, throat, nose and sinuses are expelled by Nasyam. Many diseases such as migraine, facial palsy, sinusitis, impaired olfactory sensation, tinnitus etc. are treated by nasyam.

The nose is the gateway to the brain and to consciousness. Prana, or life energy, enters the body through breath taken in through the nose. Nasal administration of medication helps to correct the disorders of prana affecting the higher cerebral, sensory and motor functions. Nasya is indicated for dryness of the nose, sinus congestion, hoarseness, migraine headache, convulsions and certain eye and ear problems.

Types of Nasya

1. Virechan (cleansing with herbal oil, powders or juice of herbs)

2. Nutritional Nasya (for vata)

3. Palliative Nasya

Nasya can be with

a. Decoctions

b. Ghee or oil

c. Powder

Substances such as calamus powder, gotu kola, onion, garlic, black pepper, cayenne, ginger, ghee oil decoctions are used in Nasya. Nasal medication should not be administered after a bath, food, sex, drinking alcohol, during pregnancy or menstruation.

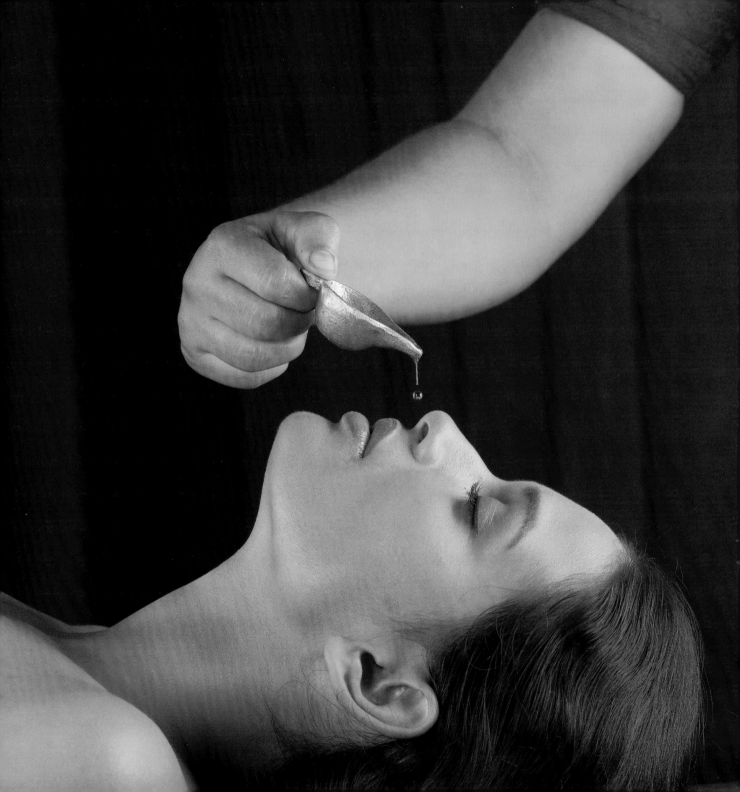

Ayurvedic Treatments in Kerala

Kerala's Ayurvedic treatment is distinct. It is a branch of Ayurveda developed by physicians in ancient Kerala from the Sodhana Chikilsa. It is a complex yet complete health program of Ayurveda that promotes fitness primarily through massages with medicated oils. The therapeutic range of Kerala treatments includes cures for ailments ranging from common low back pain to cerebral lesion diseases.

There are prescribed preparatory procedures and post treatment regimen for all intensive treatments. If these are not observed to the letter, it could lead to serious ill effects, which could be irreversible. Intense treatments demand extra care, regular checkups, specially trained people to administer and adequate space with sufficient facilities and hence hospitalisation is often recommended as nursing care and an Ayurvedic doctor's presence would be mandatory.

As Ayurvedic therapies focus on the physical and mental well being it is very effective in all type of individuals. According to Ayurveda, a healthy mind is seen only in a healthy body. Mind - body relation is well explained in Ayurveda with the simile of ghee in a pot. The heat of the pot is conducted to the ghee within it and vice versa. Mental eccentricity could lead to physical abnormalities and physical malformation to mental peculiarity. Hence, an Ayurvedic practitioner has to concurrently monitor the patient's mental and physical health. The holistic approach of Ayurveda is evident in every component of this system.

Note: The illustrated massage techniques and postures detailed in this book are directed to the masseur with the person being massaged being referred to as the subject.

Two masseurs do Ayurvedic massages in a comfortably warm room with the subject resting on a uniquely carved out wooden bed referred to as the *Droni*. However, for photographic clarity, only one masseur is shown in the pictures given.

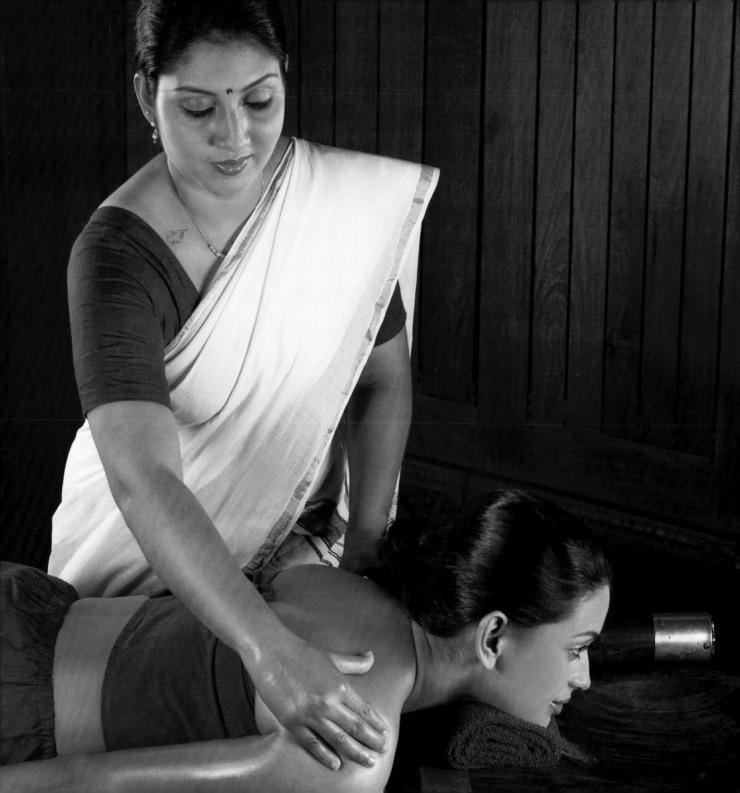

Pizhichil

Pizhichil is one among the rare and special treatments of Kerala. In this treatment, lukewarm herbal oils are applied all over the body by two to four trained therapists in a special rhythmic way continuously for about 60 to 90 minutes per day for a period of 7 to 21 days. This treatment is done in a special table made from a single piece of Strychnus nuxvomica wood. This treatment is very useful for Rheumatic diseases like arthritis, paralysis, hemiplegia, paralysis, sexual weakness, nervous weakness and nervous disorders etcetera. Pizhichil is done to get rid of the blockages in channels and nerves.

1. With the subject sitting upright, oil is liberally applied from head to toe.

2. With the subject lying down [first – face up,on the sides and then face down] apply the warm oil liberally all over the body by squeezing a linen cloth soaked in the oil in one hand and massaging with the other. Massage gently without exerting too much pressure. Heat the oil continuously to keep it warm and ensure that every inch of the body is covered. The whole process takes about 2 hours.

3. Wipe the body with a dry cloth to remove all the excess oil. Liberally apply herbal powder and wipe once again taking extra care to wipe the head dry. The subject May be made to take bath if physician allows or may be wiped well. For bath medicated (herbal) water is used.

Njavarakizhi

Njavarakizhi – It is a type of sedation process in which the whole body or any specific part there of is made to perspire by the application of certain medicinal puddings externally in the form of boluses tied up in muslin bag. Two to Four masseurs apply this for about 60 to 90 minutes per day for a period of 7-14 days. This treatment is for all types of rheumatism, pain in the joints, emaciation of limbs and certain kind of skin diseases. This is mainly to lubricate the joints and make muscles more strong.

1. Select the roots of 'Sida rhombifolia'. In two separate lots finely cut and crush the roots. Add 16 times its volume of water for each lot. Boil till only a quarter of the decoction is remaining, strain through a muslin cloth and keep aside.

2. Njavara rice is cooked in milk and Sida decoction is used.

3. Make 4 equal bundles or poultices (with muslin cloth) of the rice-herbal decoction and set aside.

4. Oil for the head should be applied and gooseberry paste over it. (Dry gooseberry is cooked in milk or butter milk is ground and used.) Apply the selected medicated oil liberally over the subject's body. The physician, depending on the physical and mental temperaments of the subject should decide the mode of application and the type of oil.

5. Soak the poultices in the second lot of the herbal concoction and in an equal quantity of milk and massage the entire body . The poultices should be comfortably warm.

6. The massage takes about 1-1.5 hours after which the rice paste is wiped off the subject's body.

7. Apply the medicated oil once again on the body. Wipe it off and bath in medicinal water according to the physician's advice.

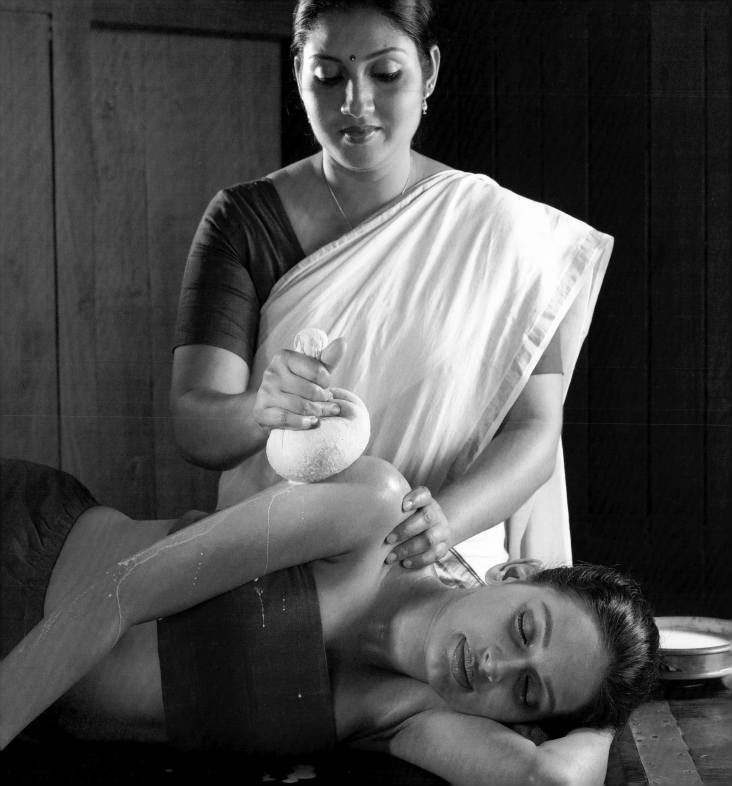

Sirovasti

Certain lukewarm herbal oils are poured into a cap fitted on the head and held for 15 to 60 minutes per day according to the patient's conditions for a period of 7 days. This treatment is highly effective for facial paralysis, dryness of nostrils, mouth and throat, severe headaches and many mental disorders.

Sirodhara

Sirodhara – Sira – means 'head' and Dhara means 'continuous flow' of a liquid. In this process some herbal oils, medicated milk, medicated butter milk etc, are poured on the forehead in a special method of about 45-60 minutes in a day for a period of 7 to 21 days. This treatment is mainly for insomnia, loss of memory, brain diseases, headaches, mental tension and certain skin diseases.

The requirements for this treatment therapy apart from the *droni* is the *Dhara Chatti* or a special vessel made of clay or an alloy of iron that does not react with the medicinal properties of the ingredients. The vessel has a hole at its centre where a wick is left hanging to permit the even flow of the contents.

1. With the subject sitting on the *droni*, apply the warm medicated oil with hands liberally on the crown.

2. Tie a *Varti* around the subject's head and knot it on the side of the head.

3. Apply liberal quantities of the medicated oil on the subjects entire body including the head and then make the subject lie down flat on the back with the head and neck resting at a comfortable angle.

4. Fill the hanging *Dhara* pot with the medicated preparations and ensure that it flows smoothly down over the wick.

5. Move the *Dhara* pot to and fro, left and right over the subject's forehead and crown. Massage the scalp with the free hand and make sure that none of the medications enter the subject's eyes.

6. The flow of medication should be uninterrupted and closely monitored at all times.

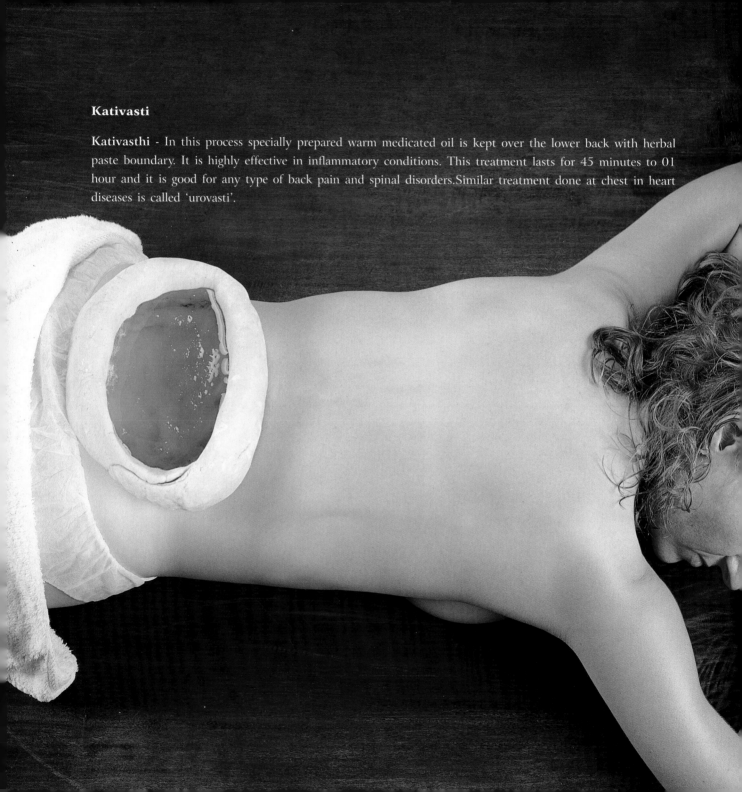

Kativasti

Kativasthi - In this process specially prepared warm medicated oil is kept over the lower back with herbal paste boundary. It is highly effective in inflammatory conditions. This treatment lasts for 45 minutes to 01 hour and it is good for any type of back pain and spinal disorders.Similar treatment done at chest in heart diseases is called 'urovasti'.

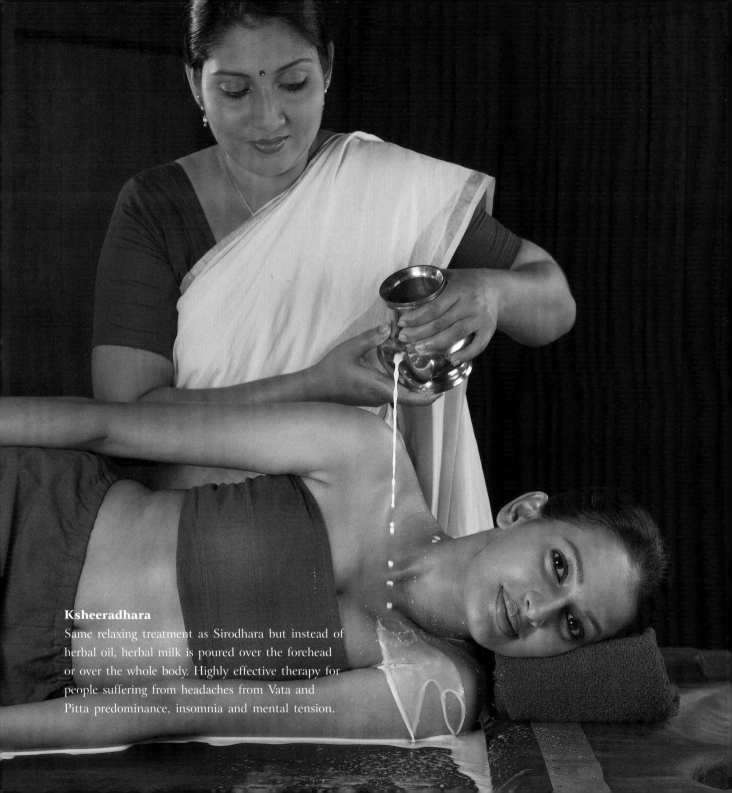

Ksheeradhara

Same relaxing treatment as Sirodhara but instead of herbal oil, herbal milk is poured over the forehead or over the whole body. Highly effective therapy for people suffering from headaches from Vata and Pitta predominance, insomnia and mental tension.

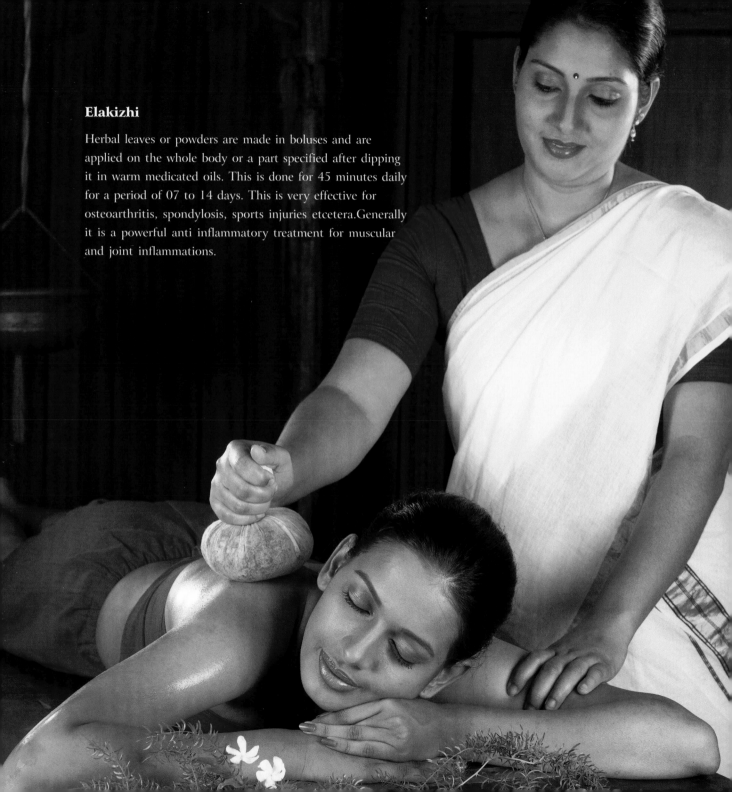

Elakizhi

Herbal leaves or powders are made in boluses and are
applied on the whole body or a part specified after dipping
it in warm medicated oils. This is done for 45 minutes daily
for a period of 07 to 14 days. This is very effective for
osteoarthritis, spondylosis, sports injuries etcetera.Generally
it is a powerful anti inflammatory treatment for muscular
and joint inflammations.

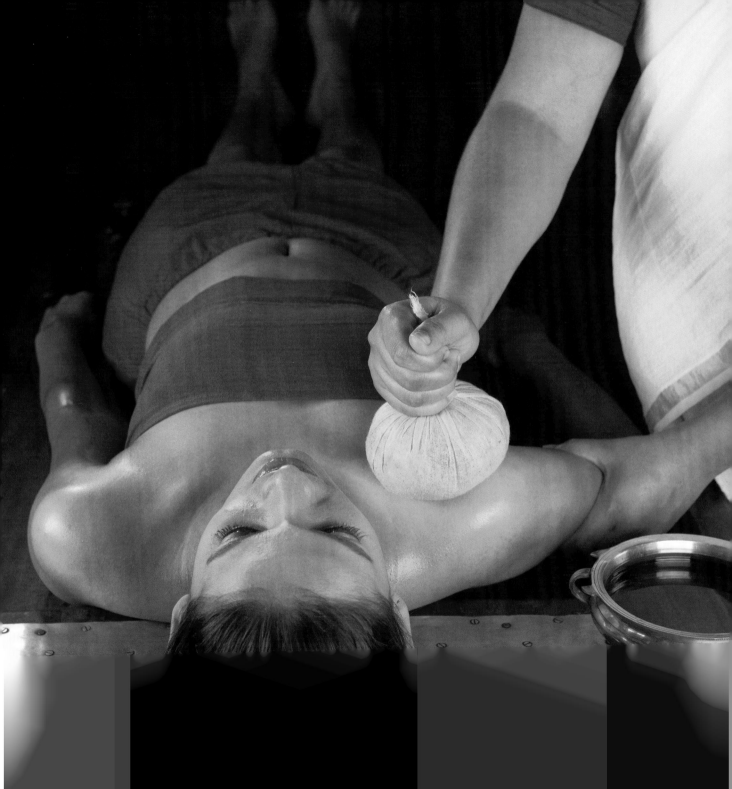

Thalapothichil

Various medicinal herbs selected according to dosha predominance is made into a paste and applied to the scalp for 30 to 45 minutes. This treatment is good for insomnia, premature greying and other problems to the hair and scalp.

1. Take seedless *Amala* or gooseberries. Soak it overnight in an earthen vessel filled with buttermilk.

2. Grind the mixture finely and set aside.

3. Liberally apply oil to the subject's head.

4. Tie a *Varti* or a comfortably tight ribbon of muslin cloth on the head immediately above the ears.

5. Firmly apply the ground mixture to the head. Primarily apply on the crown and then work to the front along the forehead, spread along the right side, along the back and finally on the left side. The thickness of application of the paste should be a uniform 3 centimetres.

6. Cover the head with a banana leaf or Lotus leaf and leave it on for at least 45 minutes.

7. Remove the banana leaf/Lotus leaf, wipe the paste off the head and have a shower.

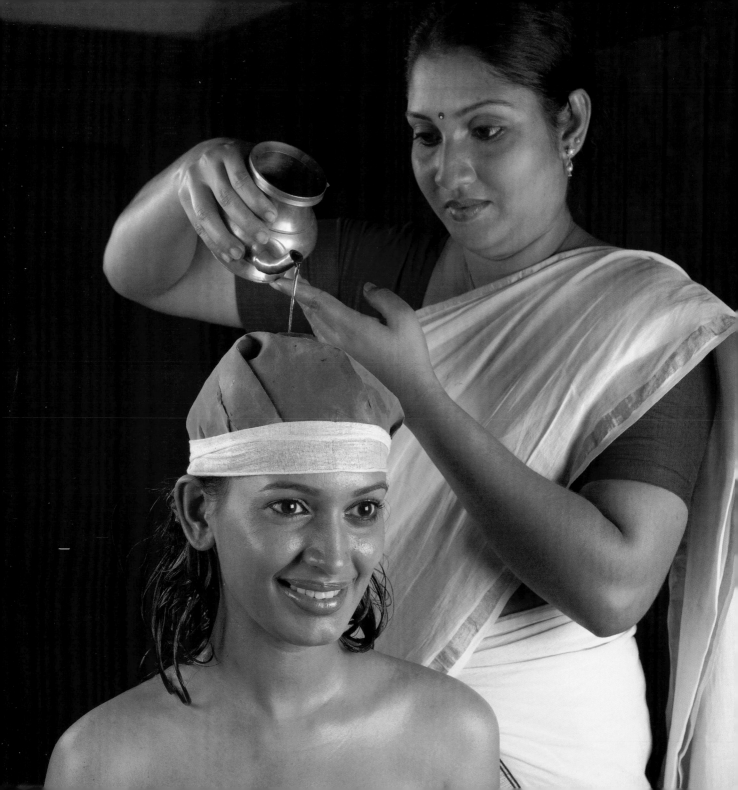

Ayurveda is excellent for all but should be administered strictly under expert supervision

Precautions

Pizhichil (oil bath) is contra - indicated in serious liver and renal problems. After each set of 7 oil baths, purgation is essential because the toxins and waste materials collected in the intestine as a result of the oil baths should be expelled, before it is reabsorbed into the body.

Blood parameters should be checked and safe levels ensured prior to commencing any intensive treatment.

Whole body rice bundle massage is contra - indicated in diabetics, obese and patients with serious cardiac, hepatic and renal disorders.

In summer, especially for patients with elevated Pitta, leaf or medicated powder bundle massage (whole body) is never recommended.

Sirodhara should not be done in cerebral thrombosis for it could lead to fatal embolisms.

Sirovasti has a strong impact on the brain. So it should be done with proper care and under the guidance and presence of a physician and only in serious
brain / nerve disorder.

Absolute rest, regular oil massages, oral drugs and peace of mind are essential throughout the curative period (after the intensive treatments) or it may affect the body negatively.

Steam bath should not be done: If you are not treated with oil inside and outside OR if you are: Obese, too lean, too weak, having loose motion (diarrhoea) or bleeding of any sort, soon after trauma, alcoholic, having cataract, skin disorders, tuberculosis, arthritis, prolapsed rectum, fatigue, anger, depression, fear, hunger, thirst, jaundice, hepatitis, anaemia, diabetes, excessive Pitta and pregnancy.